SCHOLASTIC

D1359370

Trait-Based Mini-Lessons for *Teaching Writing*

in Grades 2-4

by **Megan S. Sloan**

New York • Toronto • London • Auckland • Sydney
Mexico City • New Delhi • Hong Kong • Buenos Aires

Teaching *Resources*

To my students,
who delight me with their writing every day.

To Nora—my sister and friend.

ACKNOWLEDGMENTS

There are many people who supported me during this process and I would like to thank them.

First, to the many students who allowed their work to be shared in this book, I thank you for making the lessons "come to life."

To Sam Sebesta, Bonnie Campbell Hill, Nancy Johnson, Katherine Schlick Noe, and Ken Hermann— you have always supported and encouraged me. Sam—you know you are my favorite teacher!

To Connie Roepke, Cynthia Heffernan, Mary Ruth Thomas, and in memory of Steve Campbell, for your specific contributions.

To Kary Thome, for swapping samples and sharing stories.

To the memory of Pete Dodson, who first encouraged me to share with others.

To Linda Dobbs—I have learned much from you!

To all the staff, students, and parents at Cathcart Elementary School. What a wonderful place to teach. I am blessed to work among such professional and fun people.

To Wendy Murray, for your vision, and for beginning this whole process. To Ray Coutu, for your incredible advice and guidance. I appreciate your knowledge and expertise. To Joanna Davis-Swing and Danielle Blood—I thank you for bringing this all together. To Ruth Culham—thank you for reading this book, as an expert, teacher, and writer. Your input was invaluable. Thank you for your contributions.

To my parents, all of my family, and friends—thank you for your love and support throughout this project, and always.

Cover design by Maria Lilja
Interior design by Solutions by Design, Inc.
Interior photos by Megan S. Sloan

ISBN: 0-439-22247-8

Copyright © 2005 by Megan S. Sloan
Published by Scholastic Inc.
All rights reserved.
Printed in the U.S.A.

9 10 40 13 12

Contents

Introduction

Discovering the Traits of Writing

Years ago, I attended a writing conference at which many of the sessions focused on something I had not heard about—Six-Trait Writing Assessment. One of the presenters, a fourth- and fifth-grade teacher with incredible enthusiasm for teaching writing, had a remarkable influence on my teaching. She shared many student writing samples, showing how she helped her students improve in six areas of writing: ideas, organization, voice, word choice, sentence fluency, and conventions. She spoke about the need for defining specific criteria, assessing students' writing based on those criteria, and using this information to craft lessons. I left her presentation with a clear vision of the connection between writing assessment and instruction.

Prior to the conference, I had been teaching writing to my students on a daily, ongoing basis: we were prewriting and drafting, revising and editing, and sharing our work. But I had not been teaching my students what makes good writing—the specific characteristics of any well-written piece. They didn't have anything to shoot for because I wasn't giving them a target.

I went back to my classroom energized and ready to revamp how I was teaching writing. I recognized what was working—most importantly, that my students were writing every day. I reviewed my lessons and strategies, added to them, revised them, and began creating an atmosphere that would encourage students to love writing and to write well.

The conference helped me realize that I needed to teach specific mini-lessons on what makes good writing. First I reviewed all the writing traits—ideas, organization, voice, word choice, sentence fluency, and conventions, as well as presentation, which was later added to the traits model. I then began crafting lessons that would focus on these traits at different stages of the writing process (prewriting, drafting, revising, editing, and publishing). It wasn't as though these traits were new. The gurus of writing—Donald Graves, Lucy Calkins, Barry Lane, Donald Murray, Ralph Fletcher, Nancie Atwell, and others—had all talked about the characteristics that make a good piece of writing. And, as a reader, I knew what I liked—description and detail, vivid word choice, sentences that carried cadence, sequence and structure, and intriguing leads. But somehow, I had not been focusing my teaching on these characteristics. That was the key element missing in my teaching.

I began to plan lessons that focused on each of the traits separately, so that students could slowly start trying out new writing skills one by one. However, I knew I could not completely pull apart the traits. When a writer expands a sentence to improve the flow, she is also elaborating on an idea. By adding rich words, a writer's voice shines through. As students progressed in their skills, I planned to show the interrelatedness of the traits.

Using Familiar Strategies and Resources

In the process of developing my new writing program, I discovered that shared reading and story time provide wonderful opportunities for teaching writing. I realized that I had expert models all around me in the wonderful literature and nonfiction in my room. One of my goals is to teach students to read with a writer's eye. In order for students to write detailed descriptions or compose fluent sentences, they must hear examples of this kind of writing again and again. This exposure helps students learn to recognize what strong writing looks and sounds like. For this reason, many of my lessons include picture books and chapter books. I also encourage students to notice strong writing traits in their independent reading.

I developed other lessons that center on modeled writing. To show students that everyday happenings make interesting writing topics or that it can be a struggle to find the right word, I model the writing process again and again. In addition to using my own writing in these lessons, I use student writing to show something done well, such as an outstanding lead sentence. In addition, I invite students to help me model the process of revision or editing using their work.

I also began to use shared writing to teach the traits. With support from classmates and guiding questions from me, I have students work together to create a collaborative piece of writing. In the process, they learn specific skills, such as how to organize their writing with a clear beginning, middle, and ending, or how to expand choppy sentences to create a natural flow and rhythm. This process then becomes a model and a springboard for students when they set out to write on their own.

I found that building structure into a writing program is essential. I begin each writing period with a short mini-lesson, followed by drafting and conferring, and ending with time to share. Students do not need to take every piece of writing through the entire writing process of revising, editing, and publishing, but they do need practice at each of these stages. For this reason, I have students store their writing in folders. After I teach a lesson on revision, for example, students can pull out a piece they've already written and use it to apply the revision skills they've just learned.

As I revised my writing program, I continued to provide a scheduled time for writing every day. Without this opportunity, I've found that students lose interest in writing. They need time to write and rewrite—lots of time. I once spoke with a colleague who taught writing once a week. By the time students came back to their piece the following week, they didn't care about it anymore. There was no investment. We don't teach math only on Tuesdays and Thursdays, or reading only on Mondays, Wednesdays, and Fridays. Why should writing be any different? Why shouldn't we carve out a place for writing every day of the week, just as we do for other subjects?

Having said that, I recognize the demands of the curriculum on our classroom time. In order to provide writing opportunities every day, we must find ways to incorporate writing into the content areas—into social studies, science, and health instruction. When I have science kits delivered, for example, I plan for writing instruction to take place during my science lessons. Observing hermit crabs provides an excellent opportunity to teach a mini-lesson on word choice. As students write descriptions of their hermit crabs' appearance and movements, I encourage them to use specific adjectives and energetic verbs.

Choice is another key element of my writing program. I sometimes provide prompts and specific topics, but more often I encourage students to choose topics that are important to them. This is part of the process of helping them become proficient, independent writers. To teach a successful lesson, I don't need all my students to write on the same topic. I have found that when students are given a choice in their writing, they are more invested in the process.

I knew that with these changes, I was creating a writing environment to be proud of—one that I continue to improve upon to this day. Teaching mini-lessons on each of the writing traits helps students tackle skills a little at a time, ensuring success. Providing daily opportunities to write and giving students choice in their topics encourages them to become invested in the process. And last of all, conveying excitement and passion for writing—coupled with the belief that all students can learn to be capable writers—will make your writing program a success.

About This Book

This book includes mini-lessons for teaching the writing traits across the stages of the writing process: prewriting, drafting, revising, editing, and publishing. By changing the lessons slightly, some can be presented again and again. For example, you might present the same lesson using a different picture book as a model or by varying the topic for a piece of shared writing. The book is divided into chapters by trait. There is a chapter for each of the traits that lend themselves to the revision process—ideas, organization, voice, word choice, and sentence fluency. Conventions and presentation—the traits that fit into editing and publishing—are covered together in Chapter 6. In each chapter, you'll find an introduction to the trait, several mini-lessons and short follow-up activities, and recommended books for modeling the trait. Graphic organizers, rubrics, and other reproducibles used in the lessons are provided in the appendices. The book closes with a chapter on assessment.

As you begin your journey with the writing traits, start with ideas and organization. Build a foundation with your students, teaching them about focus, elaboration, and organization. Stay with these two traits for a while. When your students are ready, "piggyback" lessons on word choice and then sentence fluency while continuing to reinforce aspects of ideas and organization. Then add lessons on voice. Of course, conventions can be taught throughout the year—during the drafting and editing stages of the writing process. Once students have written, revised, and edited a piece that they would like to share with a wider audience, explore the qualities that contribute to effective presentation.

My hope is that you will make these lessons your own—that you will adapt them any way you see fit to make them work for you and your students. And I hope that by studying the writing traits, students will become empowered to become effective writers and enjoy the process wholeheartedly.

CHAPTER 1:

Ideas

CHARACTERISTICS OF THE IDEAS TRAIT

◎ narrow and focused topic

◎ fresh and unique ideas

◎ well-chosen details that elaborate on the main ideas

◎ accurate information

Adapted from *6+1 Traits of Writing: The Complete Guide, Grades 3 and Up* by Ruth Culham (Scholastic, 2003).

"The writing becomes beautiful when it becomes specific . . . the bigger the issue, the smaller you write."

—Ralph Fletcher, from
What a Writer Needs

As we guide students through the prewriting stage of the writing process, we become comfortable helping children generate ideas. Traditionally, teachers engage students in brainstorming topics by using word caches (such as autumn words), or recording observations shared about a common class event (such as a field trip).

While these are effective strategies, teaching ideas is about helping students see that their lives are rich with potential topics and that the concept of ideas goes beyond deciding upon a topic. Certainly, providing experiences that will help students generate writing ideas is the first step. Once they have an idea, however, how can we help students narrow their topic and develop their idea?

Encouraging the first-grade student to add one or two details to her statement

"I got a bike for my birthday" may be enough guidance for her to revise her sentence to: "I got a bike for my birthday. It is shiny and red. I rode it on my driveway." As students become more fluent writers, it is important to teach them that a clearly developed idea is not just a list of details or events.

> We went camping. We set up our tent. Then we went fishing and I caught a fish! We ate it for dinner. After dinner we went on a hike. It was fun.

Rather, the strongly developed piece will focus on one idea, such as catching the fish, and elaborate on that idea with details.

> On my first camping trip, I went fishing. I placed the bait on my hook. Then I cast my line into the river, sat down on the bank, and waited. It seemed like hours before I felt a slight tug. My whole insides were jumpy. I jolted to a stand and began reeling it in. I could see the line move closer and closer through the murky water. At last, in my view was the creature I had caught—my first fish!

A crucial aspect of developing ideas is *focus*—sticking to a topic and not wandering off. Teaching students how to focus is paramount when we teach ideas. Once they understand how to stay focused, they're ready to learn how to *show* rather than *tell* in their writing. This can be done through mini-lessons that help students learn how to elaborate, how to choose engaging details, and how to determine which information will communicate the main idea in the best way possible. This will help students learn how to paint vivid pictures with unique and memorable descriptions—a skill that serves all writers well.

The following mini-lessons strive to teach children about choosing a topic, narrowing the focus, and developing ideas at different stages in the writing process. The goal of this instruction is for students to become independent in the writing process and engaged as they write about topics that are truly meaningful to them.

What Should I Write About?
Finding a Topic

Teachers often ask me how I help students who can't think of anything to write about. If we strive to help children become independent writers, we can't always provide a topic for them. Instead, we need to teach students to decide for themselves what topics are worthy of their time and energy. How can we help them tackle the question "What should I write about?" time and time again?

I once struggled with this same question. I found my answer when I stopped creating elaborate lessons that focused on "fancy" topics and began helping students realize that their everyday experiences are worth writing about.

One way I communicate this to students is by reading aloud *You Have to Write* by Janet S. Wong, a book that explores the perpetual challenge of coming up with a topic to write about. Throughout the book, Wong shares the insecurities students might have as they try to find a topic:

> *So you look and look and look awhile for something special to write about, some magic story. . . .* Boy, how the others shine. She's got a story. She's been to France.

Wong goes on to suggest that everyone has a rich array of topics to choose from. All we have to do is look at what surrounds us in our everyday lives. She reminds us that we are the only ones who can tell our stories. Wong advises readers to "reach inside" and write about the full range of their own experiences. She urges readers to take their minds "for a walk" through their memories, starting with today and moving back in time.

After reading aloud *You Have to Write*, I ask students, "What does the author believe are the best kinds of topics?"

Several students respond, "The everyday things."

"Like what?"

Jessica says, "Like taking out the trash or walking your dog."

Emma adds, "Or how you hate to make your bed."

"I like when she wrote about her library book that got wet," says Malcolm.

"Yes," I continue, "those are all the everyday things in this child's life. Sometimes people think they have to go to Disneyland or experience an important event in order to have something to write about. But did you know the best topics are the things that happen every day, like playing soccer, reading a favorite book, or sledding down the hill at your house in the winter? What are some everyday things in your life?"

Taylor shares, "I have to set the table for dinner."

Raisha says, "I have a cat that sleeps with me."

Chase adds, "I like to play baseball."

After our discussion, I ask students to make a list of five everyday things from their lives. To help them generate ideas, I encourage them to talk with a partner about their day-to-day experiences. While students work on their lists, I compile my own list.

Once everyone has finished, I ask students to staple their lists to the inside of their writing folders so they can add to them whenever they think of new topics. Then I share my list with students.

Students compile lists of everyday topics.

POSSIBLE WRITING TOPICS

Driving to school

Reading a book

Walking my dog

Doing laundry

Taking out the trash

I "talk through" the items on my list, modeling how I decide which one I would like to write about. "I could write about how I got stuck in traffic this morning, or maybe I should write about something I love to do—like curling up on my couch and reading a book. I know, I'll write about something I don't enjoy doing but have to do every week—taking out the trash!"

Once I've decided on a topic, I write a short piece to model the next stages in the process: narrowing the topic and elaborating. Students love seeing me model the process of making ordinary topics come to life with vivid details. During the next few days, I keep my list handy so I can continue to demonstrate the process of writing about ordinary topics. Students need to see teachers write about everyday experiences, again and again, before they believe that their own everyday experiences are worth writing about.

Write a Lot About a Little
Focusing the Topic

In addition to choosing something to write about, another challenge young writers face is narrowing their topic. When writing about the zoo, they tend to write one statement about each animal. When describing a vacation, they list everything they did. Children often take on topics so large that they end up writing vague sentences with no "meat." In an attempt to write about everything, they end up writing very little of substance. It's important to make clear to students that good writing doesn't need to include everything.

To help my students understand this point, I introduce them to the idea of "writing a lot about a little." We talk about how to take a simple idea—a narrow topic—and develop it. In the course of this discussion, I teach them what it means to elaborate.

I begin by reading *The Important Book* by Margaret Wise Brown. As I turn each page, I ask students what they notice. Do they see any patterns? Students observe that each page begins with a main idea statement, lists some details, and then restates the main idea.

> *The important thing*
> *about a spoon is*
> *that you eat with it.*
> *It's like a little shovel,*
> *You hold it in your hand,*
> *You can put it in your mouth,*
> *It isn't flat,*
> *It's hollow,*
> *And it spoons things up.*
> *But the important thing*
> *about a spoon is*
> *that you eat with it.*

After reading each page I ask, "What else about _____ (spoons, daisies, grass . . .)?"

I continue reading. When we get to the page about rain, I read,

> *The important thing about rain is*
> *that it is wet.*

It falls out of the sky,
and it sounds like rain,
and makes things shiny,
and it does not taste like anything,
and is the color of air.
But the important thing about rain
is that it is wet.

I ask, "What else about rain?" Then I record student answers on a chart.

It makes puddles.
It can be hard or soft.
It falls from the sky.
It gets you wet.
Rainbows come out after it rains.
It's usually cloudy when it rains.

After completing our chart, we use the ideas to build a piece of writing.

"Okay," I begin, "if we're writing a piece about rain, we need to begin with a clear first sentence so our readers will know what our topic is. Who has an idea?"

Brian suggests, "Rain is very interesting."

I record the first sentence and ask, "Which idea from our list would you like to put next? Remember, good writers don't use everything from their idea lists."

Ally says, "I like *It falls from the sky.*" I write this sentence.

Chase suggests, "Let's put *It can be hard or soft* next." This is a perfect opportunity for me to show students how we can elaborate by combining ideas and including additional details.

I continue, "Yes, let's add that sentence and now let's read it all together." I read what we have so far:

Rain is very interesting.
It falls from the sky.
It can be hard or soft.

I share my observation that our three sentences so far are about the same length and they sound just like our list. I suggest that we change the way we start our third sentence and add some details to make our piece more interesting. To help elicit details I ask, "What do you mean, *it can be hard?*"

Jessica says, "You know, sometimes rain comes down really hard."

"That's great," I say. "Why don't we start our third sentence just like that: *Sometimes it comes down really hard.* Now how can we add a detail? What does it feel like when rain comes down that hard?"

Jesse says, "Like buckets of water are falling on you."

"Wonderful. We can combine both ideas into one sentence." I record *"Sometimes it comes down hard, like buckets of water are falling on you."* Then I say, "Now let's go back and add the part about rain being soft and elaborate on that idea by adding a detail just like we did with *It can be hard*."

James says, "How about *Sometimes it is so soft it tickles your nose?*"

"*And leaves a drip right on the end*," adds Brie.

"Wow, those are nice details," I respond. "Let me write them down." I record what students have shared and read aloud the work in progress:

> Rain is very interesting. It falls from the sky. Sometimes it comes down hard, like buckets of water falling on you. Sometimes it comes down so soft it tickles your nose and leaves a drip right on the end.

We continue like this until the group feels satisfied with our description.

> Rain is very interesting. It falls from the sky. Sometimes it comes down hard, like buckets of water falling on you. Sometimes it comes down so soft it tickles your nose and leaves a drip right on the end. Rain gets you wet. If you don't have the right clothes on you can get soppy from head to toe. If it is only sprinkling you might escape without much moisture. Rain may be a hassle, but it leaves a beautiful present when it's finished—a colorful, shimmering rainbow up in the sky!

This process allows students to see how they can take one small topic and describe it in detail to create an interesting piece of writing.

On the following day, I ask students to choose a different topic from *The Important Book*. Again, we brainstorm additional ideas about this topic and chart them. I encourage students to use this chart as they write their own pieces. We save the pieces completed by both the class and individual students for use in future revision lessons, such as adding details or revising for word choice.

Jessica composed this piece after the lesson.

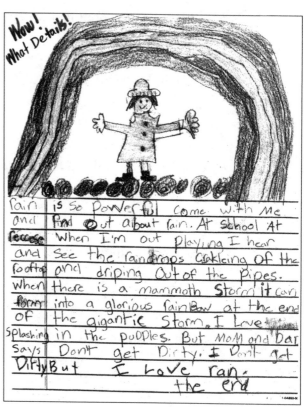

You're in the Picture:
Elaboration Through Descriptive Writing

One way to help students elaborate on an idea is to teach them how to write descriptively, which will serve them well in any genre—from persuasive pieces and informational essays to fictional stories and poetry. I begin the lesson by reminding children that they use their senses to experience the world. Description starts with the five senses, so it is important to discuss them before moving on to writing. After reviewing the senses, I ask children to use their senses as they orally describe various objects, events, and experiences.

From there, I read the book *All the Places to Love* by Patricia MacLachlan, which is filled with beautiful illustrations that realistically depict the many places surrounding a young boy's home. One of my favorite illustrations shows a small child surrounded by cattails and reeds, squatting down in the mud to inspect a turtle. The child is wearing a bright yellow raincoat, a straw hat, and red rubber boots. I open the book to this page and ask a student to hold it up so the class can look closely at the picture. Then I say, "Imagine that you are in the picture. What do you see?"

Students begin responding. Katie says, "A spotted turtle."

"Cattails," adds Bobby.

"Mud," says Taylor.

Jenny raises her hand and says, "He's wearing a straw hat."

"A grasshopper, a bird, and a puddle," responds David.

I record these in the first column of a three-column chart. I write the heading *I See* at the top of the column.

After we have compiled a lengthy list I say, "You're in the picture. What do you hear?" Again, students begin to wave their hands, eager to share.

"The squish of mud," Allie says.

"Drip, drip of rain," adds Shea.

"I hear a bird singing," says Michael.

Again, I record these ideas—this time in the second column, labeled *I Hear*.

The last question I ask is, "What do you feel?"

Rachel begins by responding, "A cool breeze."

"Cattails tickling my cheek," says Tara.

Jason adds, "Glops of mud between my fingers." I record these ideas in the third column, labeled *I Feel*. (Rather than recording responses on a chart, another option is to give students individual templates on which to record their own ideas about what they see, hear, and feel. For more of a challenge, have students also write about what they smell and taste.)

Then I explain to students that they are going to "put themselves" in this picture and write about what they see, hear, and feel. I explain that they may use ideas from our chart and encourage them to choose a few ideas, rather than all of them, to avoid ending up with a list.

To get students started I ask, "What would be a good first sentence for this piece of writing?"

Taylor suggests, "*One spring day I went for a walk.*"

"That's great. How about another idea?" I prod.

Starla raises her hand to share. "*It was a pretty spring day.*"

"Very nice. Anyone else?"

"*One rainy spring morning I was going for a walk,*" adds Courtney.

I invite students to write a first sentence that will help the reader know what the piece is about. Then I encourage them to choose one or two ideas from each of the sections of our chart and elaborate on them. For instance, I tell them, "You can start with *I see a green and yellow turtle.* Now tell what it's doing. *It is sticking out its neck and stretching. It is moving very slowly.*" By giving students this example, I model the importance of adding details to each idea. Before students begin writing, I encourage them to draw a picture of the scene they are about to describe.

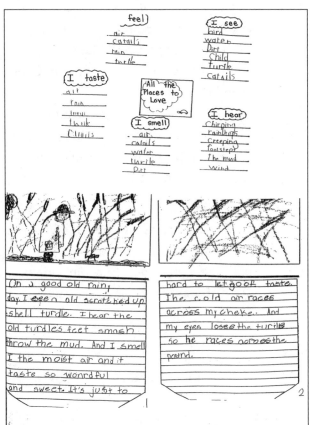

Students work together to create a sensory chart based on an illustration from a picture book. Then they "put themselves in the picture" and write their own descriptions of the place, using their senses.

Follow-Up

Give each student a copy of page 100. Invite students to choose an illustration from a picture book, put themselves in the picture, and list what they see, hear, smell, taste, and feel. Then have them write a description based on this information.

The Bare-Bones Story:
Revising for Details

Young students are often very sparse in their narrative writing. (*We went to the fair. I went on the Ferris wheel. I had cotton candy.*) These statements might be good starting points for a piece, but there comes a time to teach students how to fill in the gaps. When students aren't motivated to do so, we must find different ways to encourage them. One lesson that works for me is modeling a "bare-bones" story.

To start, I gather students around me and announce that I will tell them a story. A well-known story such as *Goldilocks and the Three Bears* works well for this lesson. In telling the story, I include only the most essential elements and leave out the details.

> Once upon a time a little girl with blond hair went out into the forest. She came upon a house. She went inside and there she saw some porridge. She ate the porridge. Then she sat in three chairs and broke one. She went upstairs and fell asleep in one of the beds. Three bears came home and chased the little girl off.
>
> The End.

I begin by asking, "What did you think of my story?"

"You forgot to tell lots of things," says Malcolm.

"Like what?" I ask.

"You forgot to tell about the porridge being too hot, too cold, and just right," Serena says.

"You forgot about how Goldilocks tried all the chairs but liked the smallest one the best," adds Emma.

Bobby raises his hand. "Goldilocks tried all three beds and fell asleep in Baby Bear's bed. His was just right."

Students continue sharing details. I record their responses on a chart and then use them to retell the story. I ask students, "Which telling do you like best, the first one or the second one?"

Many students chime in, "The second story."

"Why?" I ask.

Chase raises his hand and says, "It has more details."

"Yes, that makes it more fun to listen to," adds Taylor.

They all agree the story with the details is more interesting. I describe the first story as a skeleton with no flesh or muscle.

Emma comments, "It was just bones!"

The next day I continue the lesson by writing on chart paper something I did over the weekend:

Over the weekend I went to a concert. It was fun.

I ask students what they think of my writing. Students respond, "It's a bare-bones story. You don't have any details."

I ask them, "What else would you like to know?"

Malcolm asks, "Where was the concert?"

"Who performed?" asks Kyle.

Rachel adds, "Did you go with anyone?"

I tell students I have decided to revise my piece by adding details that will answer some of their questions. Using a red marker, I continue writing, elaborating on the original piece.

Once I've finished, I read aloud what I've written and ask students which they think is stronger, my first piece or the revised version. They all agree the revised piece is better because it includes more details and answers their questions.

Now it is time for students to revise their own writing by adding details. I redistribute pieces the students wrote the

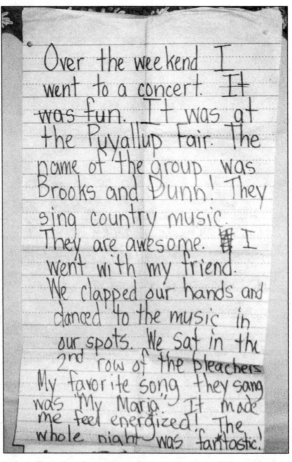

The finished piece after I modeled how to revise it for details.

morning before about something they did over the weekend. Then I pair up students and give them the following assignment:

1. Read your piece to your partner.

2. Have your partner ask you three questions that the piece did not answer.

3. Revise your piece by adding details, using the questions to guide you. Write revisions in red pencil so you can see how many details you added.

Students begin revising their writing. Afterward, they share their revised work in small groups and discuss whether the revisions improved their writing. I guide students to the understanding that adding important details is an effective way to develop the main idea of a piece.

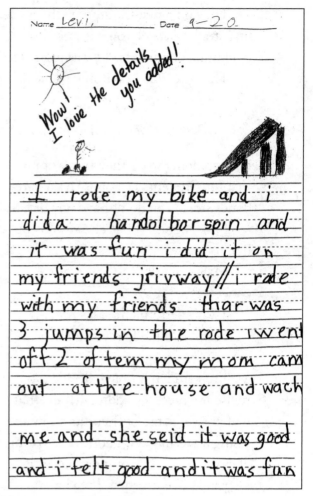

Levi's piece before the revision lesson.

Levi's revised piece.

- - - - - - - - - - -
LESSON 5
- - - - - - - - - - -

Showing Sentences
Writing to Show Rather Than Tell

Once students have learned to elaborate on their ideas by adding details, expose them to ways authors paint vivid pictures and connect with the reader. One technique I use is "showing" sentences or phrases.

I introduce the concept of showing sentences during shared reading or Read Aloud time. One of my favorite books for modeling this is Mem Fox's *Night Noises*. This story is about an old woman, Lily Laceby, and her dog, Butch Aggie, who are at home one stormy night. Unusual sounds keep waking the dog throughout the night.

I begin reading the book and stop after the description of Lily. I ask students, "What does this tell us about Lily Laceby?"

"She's old," say several students.

"How do you know she's old?"

"It said her hair was like cobwebs and her bones creaked," says Emily.

I continue probing, "Oh, does the author tell us Lily Laceby is old or show us she's old?"

"She shows us because she never says the word *old*," states Bryan.

"Yes, that's right. Good authors do that. They show us things instead of telling us. Why do you suppose they do this?"

Susanna responds, "So that we can see things and feel things better."

"That's right." I continue reading and stop again after reading:

Wind and rain rattled at the windows and trees banged against the roof.

Again I ask a question. "What's going on here?"

"There's a storm," students chime in.

"How do you know? Did the author *tell* us there's a storm?"

"No."

"That's right. She showed us. Good writers do that. They *show* us things instead of telling us. How many of you felt like you were there because of the way the author showed us the storm?"

Over the next week, I continue this exercise using different books. E. B. White presents a wonderful showing paragraph to communicate the arrival of spring in Chapter 22 of *Charlotte's Web*. Likewise in Chapter 3 of *Harry Potter and the Sorcerer's Stone*, J. K. Rowling shows, rather than tells, that a storm has hit.

Students are now ready to give it a try. I display the sentence *The girl was brave* and explain to students that this is a telling sentence. Then I ask, "Can anyone think of a showing sentence for this telling sentence? That means instead of telling us the girl is brave, you have to show us that she's brave."

Daniel responds, "The girl fought the tiger." I record his sentence.

Richelle says, "The girl took the bone from the growling dog."

Andrea shares, "The girl fell off the swing and broke her leg without crying." I record each student's idea and leave the chart up in our room.

The next day I give students the chance to write their own showing sentences. We start with the telling sentence: *The dog was fierce*. After students share some ideas, they go to work on the sentence independently. Afterward, I invite students to read their showing sentences. One of my special needs students shares, "The dog barked. He growled."

Another student with a flair for description reads his sentence, "The dog cocked his head and showed his laser-sharp teeth."

When students are ready, I encourage them to develop these showing sentences into showing paragraphs.

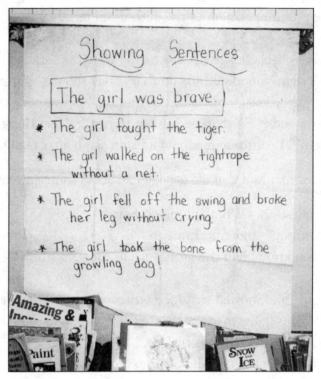

Class chart of showing sentences.

Through the gate his eyes glowed with threats. Teeth, oh his teeth were razor sharp. The ends of them flashed from the sunlight. Drool fell in globs from his mouth. His muscular arms and legs were haunched, ready to pounce. As I reached out my hand he snapped. I reached out again and he bit me.

Ally revised "The dog was fierce" into a showing paragraph.

Name _Andy_   Date _3-4_

Good authors show us things with their words.

Change this "telling" sentence into a "showing" sentence.

The dog was fierce.

Tho The dog cocked his head and showed his lazer sharp teeth.

Andy revised "The dog was fierce" into a showing sentence.

Follow-Up

Make a photocopy of the reproducible on page 101 and write a telling sentence for students to rewrite. Give students a copy of the page and encourage them to write either a sentence or a short paragraph that conveys the same information in a way that shows rather than tells.

Showing Sentences

"Wind and rain rattled at the windows and trees banged against the roof."
—*Night Noises* by Mem Fox

"A sparrow with a streaky breast arrived and sang. The light strengthened, the mornings came sooner. Almost every morning there was another new lamb in the sheepfold. The goose was sitting on nine eggs. The sky seemed wider and a warm wind blew."
—*Charlotte's Web* by E. B. White

"It was freezing in the boat. Icy sea spray and rain crept down their necks and a chilly wind whipped their faces."
—*Harry Potter and the Sorcerer's Stone* by J. K. Rowling

Ideas: Picture Books for Exploring the Trait

Fiction

All the Places to Love
  by Patricia MacLachlan

Amelia's Notebook by Marissa Moss

*Aunt Harriet's Underground Railroad in
  the Sky* by Faith Ringgold

Dandelions by Eve Bunting

Fables by Arnold Lobel

I'm in Charge of Celebrations by Byrd Baylor

The Important Book
  by Margaret Wise Brown

My Ol' Man by Patricia Polacco

Night Noises by Mem Fox

Owl Moon by Jane Yolen

The Relatives Came by Cynthia Rylant

Sitti's Secrets by Naomi Shihab Nye

Sophie and Lou by Petra Mathers

The Table Where Rich People Sit
  by Byrd Baylor

What You Know First
  by Patricia MacLachlan

When I Was Young in the Mountains
  by Cynthia Rylant

Wilfrid Gordon McDonald Partridge
  by Mem Fox

Nonfiction

Hoops by Robert Burleigh

Lightning by Stephen Kramer

Re-Zoom by Istvan Banyai

The Truth About Animal Senses by Bernard Stonehouse and Esther Bertram

Wolves by Seymour Simon

You Have to Write by Janet S. Wong

Zoom by Istvan Banyai

Biography

Eleanor by Barbara Cooney

George Washington: A Picture Book Biography by James Cross Giblin

Martin's Big Words by Doreen Rappaport

The Story of Ruby Bridges by Robert Coles

When Marian Sang by Pam Muñoz Ryan

Poetry

Extra Innings: Baseball Poems selected by Lee Bennett Hopkins

The Ocean Is . . . by Kathleen W. Kranking

Summersaults: Poems and Paintings by Douglas Florian

Winter Poems selected by Barbara Rogasky

CHAPTER 2:

Organization

> ### CHARACTERISTICS OF THE ORGANIZATION TRAIT
>
> ◎ inviting lead
>
> ◎ smooth transitions
>
> ◎ logical order of ideas
>
> ◎ effective pacing
>
> ◎ strong conclusion
>
> Adapted from *6+1 Traits of Writing: The Complete Guide, Grades 3 and Up*
> by Ruth Culham (Scholastic, 2003).

*"In every book I've written, my greatest difficulties
have been beginnings and endings. If things go wrong in the
middle I seem to be able to accept it, but the rhythm
of opening and closing lines cause me misery."*

—Mem Fox, from *Dear Mem Fox, I Have Read
All Your Books Even the Pathetic Ones*

Children are brimming with great ideas, and many of them love to write about
their ideas. Often, however, children struggle to organize their thoughts when
they write. How do we motivate students to plan a logical sequence of ideas?
How do we teach them to create opening lines that will grab the reader or
concluding paragraphs that will pull all their wonderful ideas together?

Teaching organization can be challenging, but it is so very important.
Crafting intriguing introductions, connecting ideas with transitions, ordering
ideas in a way that makes sense, controlling the pace of a piece, and ending with

a strong conclusion—these are the principles of organization. Students need many opportunities to recognize the characteristics of good organization in the books they read and then apply these characteristics to their own writing. They need to observe teachers putting the organization trait into practice. Model how to plan ideas before writing on a topic, how to organize different modes of writing, such as narrative, expository, and persuasive, and how to use transitional words or phrases so that students understand their purpose of helping a piece flow. By seeing firsthand how organization works, students will be better prepared to write their own clearly organized pieces.

In this chapter, you'll find lessons for teaching students about including a beginning, middle, and end; organizing a piece chronologically and by content; writing good leads and concluding statements; and planning their thoughts before they begin a first draft. To help children fully grasp the organization trait, it's important to teach each of these skills and then revisit them as you move on to other writing lessons. Because organization is a trait with many components, it's essential to model, discuss, and build these skills throughout the year.

LESSON 6

Reel In the Reader
Discovering Effective Leads

In any piece of writing, the lead is critical because it can determine whether or not the reader continues to read. In that first sentence or perhaps the whole first page, the author has a chance to grab the reader. Writing a good lead can be difficult for writers of all ages. Expecting students to draw in their audience with a unique and masterful opening sentence might be asking too much. At first, be content to see children begin with a clear, focused statement like *Dogs are interesting pets* or *There are many reasons to love the snow*—clear beginning sentences that let the reader know what the piece is about.

There comes a time, however, when students are ready to experiment with writing different beginnings. Before this happens, they need to be given many opportunities to discover good leads in the books they read. Shared reading and story time are great times to help students do this. Many picture books and chapter books contain excellent examples of different kinds of leads.

For the following lesson, I choose *The Escape of Marvin the Ape* by Caralyn and Mark Buehner, which features a simple yet intriguing lead: "It was feeding time, and when the zookeeper wasn't looking, Marvin . . ." I begin by asking questions about the cover and the title. After reading the first page, I pause to talk about the lead.

"What do you think? Shall we turn the page?"

Many students respond, "Yes!"

"What makes you want to turn the page? What about the picture or the writing interests you?" I ask.

Emelia raises her hand. "The gorilla is sitting with a suitcase like he's going somewhere."

"Yes, what else?"

Kyle adds, "He looks like he's twiddling his thumbs and whistling."

"I think he's waiting for the zookeeper to leave so he can escape," says Chase.

Now I direct students to the text. "How about the writing? What makes you want to turn the page?"

"Dot, dot, dot," says Serena.

"What does 'dot, dot, dot' mean?" I ask.

Malcolm responds, "It's an ellipsis. It means something's going to happen."

"Yeah, more is coming," adds Alexander.

Emma shares her observation. "It's like the author is inviting us to turn the page. She never finished the sentence. We know something is going to happen—like he's going to try to get out, but we don't know how."

"Yes," I respond, "good authors begin their books with words and pictures that make us want to turn the page and read on."

During many reading times, I share books with different kinds of leads: questions, bold statements, quotations from characters, and more. With each book, we continue the discussion about what makes a good opening. When students are comfortable with the topic, I begin using different kinds of leads in my modeled writing lessons. As I begin to write about snow, for example, I try out several different opening lines.

> I just love the snow!
> Snow is my favorite thing about winter. Let me tell you why!
> The first time I saw snow . . .

Students help me come up with the lead that I end up choosing:

> Swirls of white falling from the sky . . . it's snowing.

We decide this statement paints a vivid picture that will make readers want to read on. I am on my way.

When students are ready to put what they've learned into practice, I challenge them to experiment with different kinds of opening lines in their own writing. After studying Harriet Tubman, for example, students prepare to write a biography of this famous American. First, we work as a class to come up with three possible leads for their writing (see photo, at right). I invite students to use one of these leads or try something different as they set out to write. This kind of support continues during the next few weeks as we write about other topics. As individual students are ready, I challenge them to experiment with different kinds of opening lines in their self-selected topic writing.

As a class, students generated three leads to choose from when writing biographies of Harriet Tubman.

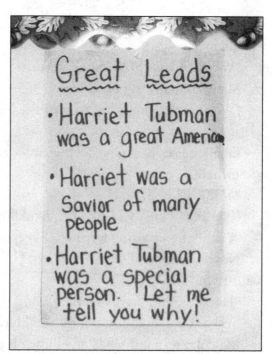

Effective Leads From Picture Books

"The Barefoot didn't see the eyes watching him as he ran onto the overgrown pathway. His breath came in great gasps. In the hours since he had run from the plantation, he had traveled faster and farther than ever in his life."
—*Barefoot: Escape on the Underground Railroad* by Pamela Duncan Edwards

"Everybody knows the story of the Three Little Pigs. Or at least they think they do."
—*The True Story of the 3 Little Pigs!* by Jon Scieszka

"The kids in room 207 were misbehaving again."
—*Miss Nelson Is Missing!* by Harry Allard and James Marshall

"Have you ever wondered about turkeys? Where are wild turkeys found and how do they live? What do turkeys eat? . . . This book answers these questions about turkeys and more."
—*All About Turkeys* by Jim Arnosky

"Out in the hottest, dustiest part of town is an orphanage run by a female person nasty enough to scare night into day."
—*Saving Sweetness* by Diane Stanley

"It should have been a perfect summer."
—*Enemy Pie* by Derek Munson

"One day, my dad looked out at the endless desert and decided then and there to build a baseball field."

—*Baseball Saved Us* by Ken Mochizuki

"Camilla Cream loved lima beans. But she never ate them. All of her friends hated lima beans, and she wanted to fit in."

—*A Bad Case of Stripes* by David Shannon

"From the beginning the baby was a disappointment to her mother. She was born red and wrinkled, an ugly little thing. And she was not a boy."

—*Eleanor* by Barbara Cooney

Effective Leads From Chapter Books

"'Where's Papa going with that ax?' said Fern to her mother as they were setting the table for breakfast.
  'Out to the hoghouse,' replied her mother. 'Some pigs were born last night.'"

—*Charlotte's Web* by E. B. White

"Once there were four children whose names were Peter, Susan, Edmund, and Lucy. This story is about something that happened to them when they were sent away from London during the war because of air-raids."

—*The Lion, the Witch and the Wardrobe* by C. S. Lewis

"'Good morning boys and girls,' the principal's voice said over the intercom. 'Please stop what you're doing and listen. I have some bad news.'"

—*Horrible Harry and the Dungeon* by Suzy Kline

"My name is India Opal Buloni, and last summer my daddy, the preacher, sent me to the store for a box of macaroni-and-cheese, some white rice, and two tomatoes and I came back with a dog. This is what happened:"

—*Because of Winn-Dixie* by Kate DiCamillo

"Just let me say right off the bat, it was a bike accident."

—*Mick Harte Was Here* by Barbara Park

"Walking back to camp through the swamp, Sam wondered whether to tell his father what he had seen."

—*The Trumpet of the Swan* by E. B. White

A Place to Begin
Developing Strong Leads

Once students understand what a good lead looks like and have had the opportunity to compose some of their own, I introduce them to more sophisticated examples. One of my favorites is from *My Ol' Man* by Patricia Polacco.

> *Whenever I get quiet and still inside and wish I was little again, all I have to do is think about my summers in Michigan. When I do this, it isn't now anymore, it is then again.*

Polacco has an effective way of reeling us in. She uses a reflective statement to transport us—back to Michigan, back to her childhood summers. We almost feel like we're there. On the first page, Polacco continues with a description of what she sees as a young girl leaning over the front porch. She makes a list: her house, "Mr. Barkoviac, trying to get the mail past the Gaffners' dog," her grandmother watering her plants in the "winderlight."

I begin my lesson by sharing the title and showing the cover, and ask students to predict what the book might be about. Then I tell them, "I'm going to read the first page. As I read, I want you to think about the way the author chose to start this story."

After reading the entire first page, I engage students in a dialogue about Polacco's lead. Students agree that this lead was longer than other leads we had previously discussed.

Serena asks, "Did this really happen?"

Emma shares, "If it didn't really happen, it sure seems like it did. The way she says, 'There's our house . . . , There's our grandma . . .'— it's like she's really remembering."

Rachel says, "It makes you want to find out about her dad, the way they were waiting for him and everything."

I ask, "Which lines from the book make you want to find out about their dad?"

"When Ritchie asks, 'Do you see him?' He seems so excited," responds Malcolm.

David notices, "The beginning part makes you think she's thinking back."

"Which words make you think that, David?"

"'When I'm quiet and still inside . . . it's not now anymore, it's then again.' I like that part."

As our conversation continues, I record student comments on a chart. Then I read the rest of the book. At the end of the story, students agree that the author created a strong lead for the book. Samantha says, "It just fit."

Next, I tell students I am going to write about something from my childhood. I decide to write about going down to the creek to play when I lived in Virginia. I begin talking about how special the creek was to me, whom I spent my time with there, and what we did when we played there. Then I begin thinking aloud as I try out possible ideas for a lead. I settle on one and write it on a chart for students to see.

> When I think of my childhood memories, one of my dearest is going down to the creek by my house in Virginia. I close my eyes and in a mere moment I am nine years old again, playing at my favorite spot.

I ask students what they think. "Do you like my lead? Are there any words you like?"

Jessica says, "I like how you talk about your memory as a 'dear memory.'"

"I like the words 'mere moment,'" observes Zach.

"What's *mere* mean?" Taylor asks.

"You know, like in just a moment," explains Emelia.

"Is there anything else you like about my lead?" I ask.

"I like how you talk about closing your eyes and then you're there, at the creek," shares Malcolm.

"Yeah, you make me want to go there," says Chase. "I want to find out what your favorite spot is."

"Well, that is what I hoped for. Good leads make the reader curious enough so they want to read on."

I encourage students to talk about cherished memories from their lives— a birthday party, a camping trip, spending time with a grandparent. I invite students to write about something from when they were younger and try out some of Polacco's techniques: painting a picture with words, creating a feeling of "thinking back," building anticipation and excitement. As they set off to write, I remind students that good authors grab us and make us want to turn the page. I encourage them to do just that.

Nonfiction Study
Organizing by Content

Now that students have practiced writing leads, I move our focus from writing an introduction to writing the middle of a piece. Over the course of a few weeks, I read nonfiction texts about animals that are organized in a variety of ways: by time (*Baby Whale's Journey* by Jonathan London), space (I share a description I wrote of an elephant, loosely based on *Seven Blind Mice* by Ed Young), and content (*Polar Wildlife* by Kamini Khanduri). We talk about the author's organizational choices and how they develop the texts.

During the last few days of our nonfiction exploration, I read aloud a few books about penguins—or I ask students to do so during independent reading. At this point, we are ready to begin our writing lesson. I start by asking students to think about the information they have learned about penguins. I partner students and ask them to record one or two facts on sentence strips. Then we randomly place these facts on a board in the room.

I give students time to read the facts and then begin the discussion by asking, "What do you notice about our facts?"

"We learned a lot!" says Jenny.

"You're right. It's amazing all the information we now know."

Ben replies, "Some facts are the same."

"Yes. Should we pile the same facts on top of each other so we are not looking at the same fact twice?" Students agree that this is a good plan.

"What else do you notice about our information?" I ask.

Trevor says, "Well, some information goes together."

"What do you mean?" I prod.

"Well, like this one says penguins dive and swim in the water and this one says they flop and slide on the ice. They both talk about how penguins move."

"You're right. Does anyone else see two facts that go together?"

Mary comes up, points to two strips, and says, "These are both about where penguins live. One says the southern hemisphere and one tells the continents penguins live on."

"I think you guys are noticing something really important. If I were to write about penguins using this information, I would want to organize the facts before I got started. Otherwise, my information would be very hard for the reader to follow. How about if we think of three or four categories that all this information fits into?"

Students decide on the following categories: *Where Penguins Live, What Penguins Look Like, How Penguins Move,* and *Interesting Facts About Penguins.* We write these headings on sentence strips and redistribute our facts to fit under each one.

Next, I tell students they are going to use these content headings to organize a paper about penguins. I remind them they will need a good lead that clearly states what their paper will be about. I explain that when we revisit the pieces later, I will help them learn how to write a good conclusion that will tie up the information for the reader.

Before we set out, Emma adds an insightful comment. "You know, we could have organized this piece by time, like start when the baby penguin was in the egg, then when it's born, and move through its life."

"You're absolutely right, Emma. We found some books that did that. That could be a choice for next time."

Using our board of facts, students begin writing.

LESSON 9

Sequence and Pacing
Organizing by Time

T o ensure that students are familiar with time as an organizational structure, over the course of a few days I read aloud texts that are written chronologically, such as biographies and other nonfiction texts, as well as historical fiction. *When Marian Sang* by Pam Muñoz Ryan, *Barefoot: Escape on the Underground Railroad* by Pamela Duncan Edwards, and *Into the Sea* by Brenda Z. Guiberson, which follows a turtle through its life, are good examples of texts organized by time.

After reading each book, I ask students how the authors organized their stories. We discuss how authors move their story through time using various devices such as dialogue, specific events, or transitional words and phrases like *after lunch, weeks passed, at 2:00* P.M., and *after a while.* We also discuss how authors use pacing and what they chose to spend the most time writing about.

On the day of the lesson, I read aloud *The Secret Shortcut* by Mark Teague, a story of two boys who are always late for school. The story follows them one day as they try to take a shortcut. After reading I ask, "What do you notice about the way the author organized his story?"

Jason answers, "Well, it starts on Monday but then the real story doesn't happen until later that week—I think on Thursday."

"You're right. Let's talk about that. Did the author spend a lot of time before the 'real story' happened on Thursday?"

Emelia raises her hand. "No. He just mentioned Monday, Tuesday, and Wednesday with a short summary of what happened on those days."

"Yes. It's important not to go on and on before you get to the meat of your story," I explain. "Otherwise, you might lose your reader. What else do you notice about the way the author moved us through the story?"

"As the boys took the shortcut, they were having a conversation," adds Emma.

"You're right. The author uses dialogue between characters to help us see the passage of time," I say.

Bobby shares, "I noticed that during the shortcut route, the boys keep reaching new places, like a jungle, then a trail, then a bridge."

"And then a mud puddle," adds Chase.

"Yes," I say, "the author uses places to mark the path to school. The story takes place throughout the week, but the 'meat of the story' takes place during the boys' walk to school on Thursday morning. Can you think of other stories we have read that are organized chronologically?"

"*Alexander and the Terrible, Horrible, No Good, Very Bad Day* happens in just one day. It starts in the morning, and then the author stops every once in a while during the day to tell another thing that happens to Alexander," shares Serena.

"You're right. Any others?"

Taylor adds, "*Dandelions* happens over weeks when they travel out West and then get settled in their new home."

"And the biography we read about Abraham Lincoln was a whole lifetime," adds Alexander.

"I am impressed!" I say. "Today, you'll have a chance to write about something chronologically. First, think of a topic from your own life—maybe a camping trip, a hockey game, or spending the night at a friend's house. Think about what happened first, next, and last. Remember, you don't want to tell every little detail! Think about the main story within your story. Let's say you spent the night at your friend's house, and during that time the dog got loose and everyone had to go look for him. If that's your 'real story,' don't spend lots of time on what happened before and after that event. Pace yourself and write just the main details. Lead up to it, spend your time working through the 'real story,' and then close your piece. Any ideas?"

"I might write about my softball game the other day," says Susanna.

"Great. That's a good one to organize by time. You might not want to write about every inning, but work us through your game. Was there an exciting part you could spend more time on?" I ask.

Johnny shares, "I could write about going to get our new dog."

"Super idea! Remember, tell the most important parts of that adventure and organize it chronologically."

I suggest that students write four or five main events during the time they are writing about. Then I have them place these events on a time line, or number them in the order they happened. This will serve as an outline.

Before students begin writing, I review transitional words and phrases with them. We brainstorm a list for them to use as a reference as they write.

Once students have finished, I ask them to share their work with partners and discuss the sequence and pacing of each story.

> **Transitional Words and Phrases**
>
> First
> Next
> After a while
> The next day
> In the morning
> Later
> Then
> While

LESSON 10

Ending on a Strong Note
Writing Conclusions

When teaching organization, I compare well-organized text to a hamburger—the lead sentence or paragraph is the top bun; the main idea is the meat; and the conclusion is the bottom bun. The pickles, cheese, onions, catsup, and lettuce are the details—the choice of words and the well-crafted sentences that add to the piece. Just as the hamburger will fall apart without that bottom bun, so will a good text fall apart without a strong ending.

I begin teaching about conclusions the same way I taught about leads: by sharing outstanding examples from books. I start with picture books, because they allow me to share many examples of conclusions over the course of a few weeks. One of the books I share is *Enemy Pie* by Derek Munson, which ends in the following way:

> *As for Enemy Pie, I still don't know how to make it. I still wonder if enemies really do hate it or if their hair falls out or their breath turns bad. But I don't know if I'll ever get an answer, because I just lost my best enemy.*

When I ask students what makes this an interesting ending, Malcolm responds, "He still has questions left about Enemy Pie."

"Yeah, he kind of sums up what it was supposed to do, but now his enemy is his friend, so he'll never know," adds Emma.

"Yes, and we feel as though his problem has been solved, don't we?" I add. Later that week I read *Jumanji* by Chris Van Allsburg, which concludes:

> *Both children answered, "I hope so," but they weren't looking at Mrs. Budwing. They were looking out the window. Two boys were running through the park. They were Danny and Walter Budwing, and Danny had a long, thin box under his arm.*

"What do you think of this ending?" I ask.

"It's funny," says Chase.

"What makes it funny?"

"Well, the boys have the Jumanji game in their hands and now they're going to have the trouble," answers Rachel.

"How do you know it's the Jumanji game?" I prod.

"Because even though it doesn't say so, you know it's a long, thin box and that's the shape of the Jumanji box," Emelia explains.

"Yes," I add, "we get a little laugh at the end, don't we?"

The next day I read *Egypt* by Stephen Krensky and I focus on the last line.

> *The Nile River remains as important to Egyptians today as it was to their ancestors, who created a civilization that lasted for almost 3,000 years.*

After reading, I ask, "What do you notice about this ending?"

"It sort of restates the most important idea," says Serena.

"It links today to a long time ago," adds Bobby.

"Yes, sometimes authors just restate an important thought to end their piece or they summarize what has already been said. Restating or summarizing is another effective way to conclude a piece of writing."

I ask students to take out their nonfiction pieces on penguins that they wrote during a previous lesson. I explain that they are going to have a chance to go back and write an effective conclusion for their piece. I encourage students to use the technique of restating or summarizing the most important idea by making an important general statement about penguins.

I begin, "Sometimes we can look at our lead sentence or paragraph and borrow a word or two to use in our concluding statement. Would anyone like to share their lead?"

Kyle shares, "Penguins are fascinating creatures."

"That's great, Kyle. Your lead is a general statement that could also be written in a different way and used as a concluding statement. Anyone else?"

Trevor raises his hand. "They live in the icy water, eat krill, and even though they don't fly, these animals are birds. Can you guess what they are?"

"Another good idea. You started with some facts and a question. What words or phrases could you borrow from this lead to put in your conclusion?"

Trevor answers, "Maybe *birds* and *don't fly* or *animals*."

I send students off to reread their penguin pieces and write concluding statements, reminding them to think of ways to either summarize or restate an important idea.

BOBBY'S CONCLUSION:

Although penguins look like little men in tuxedos, they are really just birds living in the southern part of our earth, trying to have fun and survive.

Different Types of Conclusions From Picture and Chapter Books

An Important Idea Restated or Summarized

"Now you've heard of the jazz-playin' man. The man with the cats who could swing with his band.

        King of Keys.
           Piano Prince.
              Edward Kennedy Ellington.
                The Duke."

—*Duke Ellington* by Andrea Davis Pinkney

"But the good part is I saved Shiloh and opened my eyes some. Now that ain't bad for eleven."

—*Shiloh* by Phyllis Reynolds Naylor

A Challenge to the Reader

"Today there are only around 20,000 of us left. We enjoy our life in the rain forest. Please don't take it away. Do what you can to protect us. Our survival depends on you."

—*Orly the Orangutan* by Jon Resnick

Something Learned

"Jack felt a surge of happiness. There's another kind of everyday magic, he thought, the magic of family.

    In that moment, it seemed like the best magic of all."

—*High Tide in Hawaii (Magic Tree House #28)* by Mary Pope Osborne

Personal Observation

"It is not often that someone comes along who is a true friend and a good writer. Charlotte was both."

—*Charlotte's Web* by E. B. White

Humor

"Both children answered, 'I hope so,' but they weren't looking at Mrs. Budwing. They were looking out the window. Two boys were running through the park. They were Danny and Walter Budwing, and Danny had a long, thin box under his arm."

—*Jumanji* by Chris Van Allsburg

A Look Into the Future

"Decisions were delightful after the curse. I loved having the power to say yes or no, and refusing anything was a special pleasure. My contrariness kept Char laughing, and his goodness kept me in love.

And so, with laughter and love, we lived happily ever after."

—*Ella Enchanted* by Gail Carson Levine

A Promise for the Future

"'We'll be back to run it again.' And I knew that it was true."

—*Woodsong* by Gary Paulsen

Life Continues

"Slowly she slipped off her tennis shoes and looked down at her feet, which were dyed blue. Then she got up quickly and went to get ready for the party."

—*The Summer of the Swans* by Betsy Byars

Organization: Picture Books for Exploring the Trait

Fiction

Aunt Isabel Tells a Good One by Kate Duke

Barefoot: Escape on the Underground Railroad by Pamela Duncan Edwards

A Chair for My Mother by Vera B. Williams

Dear Mr. Blueberry by Simon James

Diary of a Wombat by Jackie French

Enemy Pie by Derek Munson

The Great Kapok Tree by Lynne Cherry

Hey, Little Ant by Phillip and Hannah Hoose

I Am the Dog, I Am the Cat by Donald Hall

In the Small, Small Pond by Denise Fleming

My Great-Aunt Arizona by Gloria Houston

My Ol' Man by Patricia Polacco

The Mysteries of Harris Burdick by Chris Van Allsburg

The Sun, the Wind and the Rain by Lisa Westberg Peters

Train to Somewhere by Eve Bunting

Tuesday by David Wiesner

Willy the Wimp by Anthony Browne

Wings: A Tale of Two Chickens by James Marshall

Nonfiction

All About Turkeys by Jim Arnosky

Baby Whale's Journey by Jonathan London

If You Lived in Colonial Times by Ann McGovern

Into the Sea by Brenda Z. Guiberson

Look to the North: A Wolf Pup Diary by Jean Craighead George

Penguins! by Gail Gibbons

The Tortilla Factory by Gary Paulsen

Walk With a Wolf by Janni Howker

Biography

Duke Ellington by Andrea Davis Pinkney

Just a Few Words, Mr. Lincoln: The Story of the Gettysburg Address by Jean Fritz

A Picture Book Biography of Helen Keller by David A. Adler

Thank You, Sarah! The Woman Who Saved Thanksgiving by Laurie Halse Anderson

Poetry

Hiawatha's Childhood in *The Song of Hiawatha* by Henry Wadsworth Longfellow

A Poke in the I: A Collection of Concrete Poems selected by Paul B. Janeczko

Sea Watch: A Book of Poetry by Jane Yolen

Winter Poems selected by Barbara Rogasky

Picture Books With Different Organizational Structures

Time: Circle Story

Free Fall by David Wiesner

Ocean Tide Pool by Arthur John L'Hommedieu

The Tortilla Factory by Gary Paulsen

Time: One Day

Alexander and the Terrible, Horrible, No Good, Very Bad Day by Judith Viorst

The Great Kapok Tree by Lynne Cherry

Red Wolf Country by Jonathan London

Sarah Morton's Day: A Day in the Life of a Pilgrim Girl by Kate Waters

Journey/Passage (day, week, rainstorm, hour, weeks, season, year)

Barefoot: Escape on the Underground Railroad by Pamela Duncan Edwards

A Chair for My Mother by Vera B. Williams

A Desert Scrapbook by Virginia Wright-Frierson

In November by Cynthia Rylant

Train to Somewhere by Eve Bunting

Life's Journey

George Washington: A Picture Book Biography by James Cross Giblin

Into the Sea by Brenda Z. Guiberson

A Picture Book Biography of Helen Keller by David A. Adler

Diaries

Diary of a Wombat by Jackie French

Look to the North: A Wolf Pup Diary by Jean Craighead George

Space

All the Places to Love by Patricia MacLachlan

Barnyard Banter by Denise Fleming

One Leaf Rides the Wind by Celeste Davidson Mannis

Time and Space

Meanwhile, Back at the Ranch by Trinka Hakes Noble

Seven Blind Mice by Ed Young

The Sun, the Wind and the Rain by Lisa Westberg Peters

Content

All About Turkeys by Jim Arnosky

Amazing Beetles by John Still

A Freshwater Pond by Adam Hibbert

Life in the Polar Lands by Monica Byles

CHAPTER 3:

Voice

CHARACTERISTICS OF THE VOICE TRAIT

◎ interesting tone that suits the purpose and audience

◎ strong connection between the reader and writer

◎ passion for the topic (expository and persuasive writing)

◎ sincere and engaging text (narrative writing)

◎ language that reveals the writer

Adapted from *6+1 Traits of Writing: The Complete Guide, Grades 3 and Up* by Ruth Culham (Scholastic, 2003).

---

*"Voice is the imprint of the person on the piece . . .
As writers compose, they leave their fingerprints all over their work."*

—Donald Graves and Virginia Stuart, from
Write From the Start

I once began a teacher workshop on voice by asking participants what they usually do when they finish a good book. Among the answers was, "I pass it on for someone else to read." When I asked why, they didn't say, "Because it is so well organized." Instead, what makes us recommend a book is its voice.

Teaching students to write with voice can be difficult because it is a unique reflection of the writer. The best way we can help students discover their own voices is to define the concept for them, help them recognize voice in different kinds of writing, and encourage them to look for and speak with their own voice when they write.

Unfortunately, there is no neatly defined "right answer" when it comes to how to write with voice. Why? First of all, different people view voice in different ways. In a workshop, I once read Mem Fox's *Tough Boris* to show that even a simple book can have a strong voice. Afterward, a teacher asked me why I chose this book. Even after I explained my thinking, she disagreed. The book did not touch her as it had touched me.

I loved *Angela's Ashes* by Frank McCourt. Having grown up Irish Catholic, I could relate to some of the feelings and events described in this memoir. While it was a tragic story, I found humor in the tellings of this young boy's life in Ireland. I think that is what the author intended. However, while there are those who share my opinion, many find it to be a depressing book. While I hear humor mixed with sadness in the author's voice, other readers might hear only sadness.

Each book is filtered through the individual reader's lens. Our experiences and interests affect our opinions of the books we read. What speaks to one person can be irrelevant to another. One reader might really enjoy a book about basset hounds, for example, while another might not find it interesting at all. That doesn't mean, however, that the piece isn't filled with voice; it just means one reader doesn't care about the topic as much as the other.

Add to this that different kinds of writing call for different voices, and it becomes clear that voice is a complicated subject. While descriptive writing may be a wonderful way to transport readers to an unfamiliar place, it may not be the best way to communicate how to run a particular computer program. The purpose of the two pieces is different, and so is the audience. In one, the author might pull the reader in, taking time to zoom in on small details. In the other, the writer conveys directions quickly and simply, anticipating the needs of the reader. Although different in many ways, both pieces can still have voice. By considering the audience and purpose, a writer develops a tone that fits the piece. Naturally, different kinds of writing will convey different voices.

When reading aloud to children, try to communicate the author's intent so that it will be easier for them to recognize the story's voice. Is the author trying to make the reader laugh, cry, reflect, care, or become informed? Whatever the case, the author who writes with voice writes with conviction and authority and connects with the reader throughout the piece.

When crafting writing lessons, we need to consider how to encourage students to write with voice. Teaching students how to establish their purpose and audience, how to choose topics they care about, and how to connect to their readers will allow young writers to find their own voice. The lessons in this chapter are designed to provide that kind of instruction.

When it comes down to it, voice is the essence of a piece of writing. As Donald Murray says, "Voice separates writing that is read from writing that is not read . . . . Voice is the writer revealed."

Voice Olympics
Rating Papers for Voice

The idea for this lesson came from my colleague Steve Campbell, who created it during the 1998 Nagano Olympic Games. To introduce the lesson, I distribute photocopies of the scoring guide on page 102 adapted from one in *6+1 Traits of Writing: The Complete Guide, Grades 3 and Up* by Ruth Culham (Scholastic, 2003). We discuss the guide and talk about the attributes of voice listed on it. I then share several anonymous short pieces with varying degrees of voice. (A good source for student writing samples is the Northwest Regional Educational Laboratory Web site—www.nwrel.org. Or you might write your own pieces.) Using the scoring guide, students rate the papers 1 to 5 for their use of voice. I engage students in a discussion about each paper and the class agrees on a score for each. These papers then become benchmarks for the class.

On the following day, I divide the class into groups of four and announce that we will be playing a game called the Voice Olympics. I give each group five pieces of 9- by 12-inch tagboard and have them write a number 1 to 5 on the boards. I also give each group the scoring guide for reference.

Next, I display an overhead transparency of an anonymous student paper (obtained from the NWREL Web site) and read it aloud. Once I have finished, I give groups time to huddle together, discuss the paper, and decide on a score. When I ring a bell, groups hold up a score for the paper. If there is a difference of opinion, groups defend their score, using language from the scoring guide.

Students absolutely love this fun approach to learning the attributes of voice. It encourages them to study the scoring guide and interact with classmates. They have an opportunity to see what voice really means. For young writers, recognition of voice is the first step in learning how to use voice in their writing.

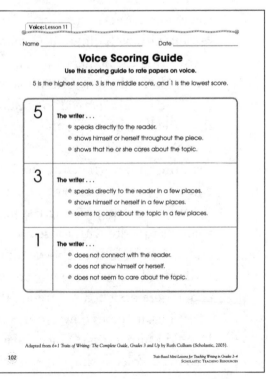

Voice: Lesson 11

Name _____   Date _____

Voice Scoring Guide

Use this scoring guide to rate papers on voice.

5 is the highest score, 3 is the middle score, and 1 is the lowest score.

5   The writer . . .
- speaks directly to the reader.
- shows himself or herself throughout the piece.
- shows that he or she cares about the topic.

3   The writer . . .
- speaks directly to the reader in a few places.
- shows himself or herself in a few places.
- seems to care about the topic in a few places.

1   The writer . . .
- does not connect with the reader.
- does not show himself or herself.
- does not seem to care about the topic.

Adapted from *6+1 Traits of Writing: The Complete Guide, Grades 3 and Up* by Ruth Culham (Scholastic, 2003).

102   *Trait-Based Mini-Lessons for Teaching Writing in Grades 2–4*
SCHOLASTIC TEACHING RESOURCES

Strong Voice and Weaker Voice
Comparing Two Texts

Sometimes the best way to explain something is by showing an example of what it looks like and what it doesn't. One of my favorite ways to help students understand voice is by reading two versions of the same story or two texts on the same subject—one full of voice, the other without much at all.

During a unit on folk or fairy tales, I read aloud two dramatically different versions of *Goldilocks and the Three Bears*. I start with a very simple version, such as this one:

> *There once was a little girl named Goldilocks. One day she took a walk in the forest. Goldilocks saw a house and went in. She found three bowls of porridge. One was cold. One was hot. One was just right.*

After reading the story, I encourage students to share how it makes them feel. These are typical responses:

◎ It was kind of boring.

◎ It didn't have interesting words.

◎ There weren't a lot of details.

I then read James Marshall's version of the fairy tale, which is a rich and humorous retelling. After reading, I ask students what they think of this version. Students respond with the following comments:

◎ It was funny.

◎ I laughed a lot.

◎ There were more details.

◎ This book was more fun to listen to.

◎ I really liked the pictures.

As we compare the two versions, I encourage students to identify what made them prefer James Marshall's retelling.

I ask, "What was funny about this book?"

Ben jumps right in. "The characters said funny things."

"Like what?" I ask.

Katie says, "When Goldilocks said, 'They must have kitties' when she saw all the hair."

I ask her to explain. "Why was that funny?"

Katie continues, "Because it was the bears' hair."

"So when the author has the character say funny things, do you like the book better?" I ask.

Many students respond, "Yeah."

I continue, "How about the narrator? How many of you thought the storyteller was almost like a character? The narrator had a distinct voice, didn't he?" Several students nod. "How about the details? Johnny, you said this version had more details than the other one. Which details stood out to you?"

Johnny answers, "Well, it said Goldilocks was going to buy muffins. The other book didn't tell us why she was in the woods."

Bobby adds, "Yeah, and when she broke the chair, the author told us she rocked and rocked until the chair fell apart."

Students agree they would recommend the second version but not the first. I conclude the discussion by explaining that the difference between the two books—everything they noticed—is that the second book is filled with voice. This is what makes a story memorable and unique and this is why we tend to recommend one book over another.

Follow-Up

On another day I read aloud a nonfiction book about ants—one that is not written in a memorable style but provides a lot of information. Later that day, I read Steve Parker's *It's an Ant's Life: My Story of Life in the Nest*. This book also supplies a wealth of information, but it presents the story from the ant's point of view. It starts out:

> *Meet me: I've got a few minutes to spare, so I can finally start my journal. Some of us have been given a short rest from work. But like all ants, I like to stay busy, so I've only got time for a few facts about me and my friends.*

Pictures, diagrams, and article excerpts accompany the narrative. Students unanimously agree that Parker makes learning about ants fun. They conclude that this book is a great example of a voice-filled text.

In the following days and weeks, we read a number of "voice-filled" books. Together, we create a chart of comments that relate to voice, such as:

◎ It's interesting.

◎ It can make you laugh or feel something deep.

◎ You relate to it.

◎ The voice can depend on the kind of writing.

◎ The author seems to know what he or she is talking about.

As we discuss the texts and add to this list, students learn how to define voice, as well as how to recognize it and appreciate it in the books they are reading. They are on their way to understanding a concept that will help them make their writing unique.

LESSON 13

From the Shoe's Point of View
Giving Inanimate Objects Voice

One way I prepare children to write fictional pieces with voice is by encouraging them to view stories through various characters' eyes. Everyone loves hearing the story of *The Three Little Pigs* from the wolf's point of view or *The Three Billy Goat's Gruff* from the troll's perspective. I begin a series of mini-lessons by reading these stories and discussing point of view.

Then I bring out four very different shoes—a cowboy boot, a high-heeled shoe, a beat-up sneaker, and a beach sandal. The students and I talk about the individual experiences these shoes might have had and what each shoe might have to say to one another. We discuss the attitudes, likes, and dislikes each might have if it were alive. I invite four students to "be one of the shoes" and say something to one or more of the others.

For example, Brooke, the high-heeled shoe, says to Daniel, the beat-up sneaker, "My life is so busy. I have so many parties to attend. You couldn't possibly understand."

Daniel responds, "Just because you're fancy doesn't make you better than me. My life has been hard. My owner always wears me in the dirt and mud. I bet no one wears you out in the rain."

The "shoes" continue their conversation while other students provide ideas. This activity serves as an effective prewriting activity for the following prompt:

> Choose one of the shoes. Tell another shoe about your life.
> Include the good and the bad things about being that shoe.

Students have a wonderful time writing to this prompt. Once they have finished writing, they share their pieces and we discuss how each writer used a different voice. Students have an easy time recognizing the voice emerging in each piece.

Follow-Up

Following the shoe activity, I give students these other point-of-view prompts based on inanimate objects:

You are a _____. Tell _____ about your life.

A pencil talking to a piece of paper

A computer talking to its owner

A sock talking to a shoe

A shoe talking to a hat

A playground ball talking to some students

A baseball talking to a bat

A jump rope talking to a child

Boy, what a life. Always being put on and getting covered with mud and dirt, snow, rain, and getting brushed until I could get up and walk.

Well, don't laugh. Picture yourself being thrown in the closet, stomped on, being sent to the repair shop and getting nails driven into yourself. Every single day, tromped on and getting thrown around the room. My back is aching and my twin's isn't any better. He gets everything I get. Every morning getting tied up so tight that I could turn blue, and so could my brother. And who knows where my other brother and four sisters are. And my mom and dad are undoubtedly in the trash.

Yeah, now you know how I feel. I envy you so much, you lucky hat.

By Tom

Tom describes a shoe talking to a hat.

Book Reviews
Finding a Voice to "Sell" a Book

(M)ost of my students love to read. They enjoy talking about what they've read during literature circles and partner reading times and they like recommending books to their classmates. I find that children get closer to their "natural voice" when they are expressing their opinions and interests, so writing book reviews offers an effective way to foster voice.

Many of my students have seen the book reviews at the end of episodes of *Reading Rainbow*. I record a few of these and show them in class to launch a discussion of what makes a book review. After watching several reviews, students brainstorm a list of "ingredients" for a book review. We record these on a chart:

◎ Names the book and author.

◎ Tells the main idea of the book.

◎ Doesn't give away the ending.

◎ Tells why the reviewer liked the book.

◎ Tells if it was funny.

◎ Tells about the characters.

◎ Describes the pictures.

◎ Tells why others should read the book.

After this, I share a few age-appropriate reviews from local papers of books for adults, as well some children's book reviews from *The Reading Teacher*. In addition, I model writing my own book review of *It Came From Beneath the Bed!* by James Howe, which I just started reading to the class.

> Have you ever wondered what authors do to get published? How do they feel? What challenges do they face? *It Came From Beneath the Bed!* by James Howe is about Howie Monroe. Howie is a dachshund puppy whose Uncle Harold wrote the Bunnicula Books. Howie wants to be a published writer just like his uncle, but he's finding out that this writing business is not so easy. Howie will make you laugh as he uses every positive adjective in the dictionary to describe himself. Find out who Delilah is, why she keeps getting so mad at Howie, and what part she plays in solving the mystery of *It Came From Beneath the Bed!*

We read aloud this review and talk about what parts were effective. Brie mentions, "I like how you started with a couple of questions. That made us wonder things."

Joe adds, "You gave us a little information but you didn't give away the whole book. We don't know how it ended."

"I want to know who Delilah is," says Tara.

I then ask students to think about a book they really enjoyed reading and would like to review. Before students begin to write, I remind them to refer to our list of ingredients.

As students write, I confer with them and provide help as needed. For example, some students may need support in ending with a strong sentence or not "giving the book away." Once students have finished, I have them read aloud their pieces and then we post the reviews in the hallway for other classes to enjoy.

BOOK REVIEW

Encyclopedia
TITLE
REVIEWED BY: Zachary

If you like KnawleDge the Encyclopedia is the book for you! so the more you read the smarter you get, so read the Encyclopedia the biggest book on earth!

Zach reviews the encyclopedia.

Book Review

Book Title: Mick Harte Was Here By Barbara Park

Mick Harte Was Here is a great book! It starts out giving you the impression that something is really wrong. You keep reading as Mick's sister tells the story, and believe me, before you know it you only have a few pages left. The end is a real surprise! READ IT!

Reviewed by: Joe

Joe reviews Mick Harte Was Here by Barbara Park.

Voice: Picture Books for Exploring the Trait

Fiction

All the Places to Love by Patricia MacLachlan

The Bee Tree by Patricia Polacco

Diary of a Wombat by Jackie French

Fly Away Home by Eve Bunting

Goldilocks and the Three Bears by James Marshall

Martha Speaks by Susan Meddaugh

Miss Nelson Has a Field Day by Harry Allard

My Ol' Man by Patricia Polacco

Pink and Say by Patricia Polacco

The Stinky Cheese Man and Other Fairly Stupid Tales by Jon Scieszka and
    Lane Smith

Tough Boris by Mem Fox

Train to Somewhere by Eve Bunting

Willy the Wimp by Anthony Browne

Nonfiction

Fabulous Frogs by Linda Glaser

Hoops by Robert Burleigh

It's an Ant's Life: My Story of Life in the Nest by Steve Parker

Koko's Kitten by Francine Patterson

The Moon Book by Gail Gibbons

Penguins! by Gail Gibbons

Sharks by Seymour Simon

Where Once There Was a Wood by Denise Fleming

Biography

A Brilliant Streak: The Making of Mark Twain by Kathryn Lasky

Marco Polo by John Riddle

Monet by Mike Venezia

Sadako and the Thousand Paper Cranes by Eleanor Coerr

Thank You, Sarah! The Woman Who Saved Thanksgiving
    by Laurie Halse Anderson

Poetry

Heartsongs by Mattie J. T. Stepanek

Honey, I Love and Other Love Poems by Eloise Greenfield

Insectlopedia: Poems and Paintings by Douglas Florian

Love Letters by Arnold Adoff

Marvelous Math: A Book of Poems selected by Lee Bennett Hopkins

Something on My Mind by Nikki Grimes

CHAPTER 4:

Word Choice

> ### CHARACTERISTICS OF THE WORD CHOICE TRAIT
>
> ◎ precise, powerful, and natural language that makes the meaning clear
>
> ◎ energetic verbs and carefully chosen nouns and modifiers
>
> ◎ unique and memorable phrases
>
> ◎ vivid description
>
> Adapted from *6+1 Traits of Writing: The Complete Guide, Grades 3 and Up* by Ruth Culham (Scholastic, 2003).

"The difference between the right word and nearly the right word is the same as that between lightning and the lightning bug."

—Mark Twain

I love words. I love the power just one word can have over a sentence. When I teach vocabulary in any subject area—reading, math, science, or social studies—I find the same enthusiasm in my students. Our shared passion for words makes word choice my favorite trait to teach. As we come across powerful and unique words, we add them to a word wall. Students eagerly search for words in their own reading to add to our collection.

As I teach lessons on word choice, I find that students immediately "get" it. They find this trait easier to understand and apply than ideas, organization, or voice—perhaps because it is more tangible. Young writers seem to naturally understand how to revise for word choice. Recently Emily, a second-grader in my class, asked another student, "What's another word for *shine?*"

The child responded, "How about *sparkle* or *glisten?*"

On another day, Joey used our class chart to help him change the word *walk* to *stroll.* Young writers quickly grasp the power of replacing ordinary words with extraordinary ones.

Exploring word choice provides students with a deeper understanding of words. It gives them the resources to expand their vocabularies. For example, while Sarah was sharing a photograph of a horse during her week as class VIP (Very Important Person), she told her classmates, "Horses are my hobby."

Teddy raised his hand and asked, "What's a hobby?"

She thought about it and replied, "You know, it's my passion."

Teddy nodded with understanding.

A few weeks earlier we had read Petra Mather's *Sophie and Lou,* a story about a mouse whose passion for dancing helps her overcome her shyness. Even though the author had not used *passion* in her writing, we spoke about that word when we discussed the character's love for dancing. Sarah's connection of the words *hobby* and *passion* was fascinating to me, as was Teddy's immediate grasp of her sophisticated definition. They were displaying a new level of discourse about language, a result of our study of word choice. I was not the only one to notice the students' development; parents began asking what I was doing to expand their children's oral vocabulary.

Through focused mini-lessons, students become empowered and begin putting into practice all that they are learning about good writing. One day during Writer's Workshop, before we began mini-lessons on word choice, I asked students to use an interesting word in their writing. Ben wrote about Thanksgiving. While he included many details, his words were very ordinary.

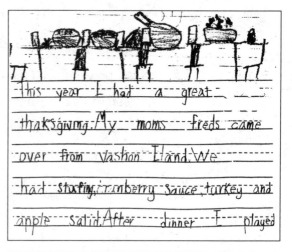

Ben's writing in December.

This year I had a great Thanksgiving. My mom's friends came over from Vashon Island. We had stuffing, cranberry sauce, turkey, and apple salad. After dinner I played with my mom's friend's kids Trevor and Liza. Then we went into the garage. We hit the piñata. My big brother Gabe smashed it open. I didn't get very much candy. My mom's friends stayed overnight. In the morning we had breakfast. After breakfast my mom's friends went home. I had a great Thanksgiving.

When he circled *great* as the interesting word he used, I knew I had work to do. For the next six weeks, I taught a series of mini-lessons focusing on word choice. At the end of the six weeks, Ben wrote a story about a Dungeness crab named Doug. Here's an excerpt:

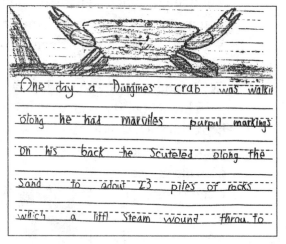

One day a Dungeness crab was walking along. He had marvelous purple markings on his back. He scuttled along the sand to about 23 piles of rocks, which a little stream wound through to reach the ocean. Doug lay down in a shallow end of the stream. Then he said to himself, "I think I will walk a little further down the river and see if I can find some minnows for lunch." He waddled behind a pile of rocks. Soon a school of seven minnows darted into a clump of seaweed not far away. He advanced closer to the seaweed. Then he launched himself into the seaweed. The minnows scattered in all directions . . .

The effect the lessons had on Ben was clear. He was able to see that good authors choose powerful words—and that he could do the same. Through our study of word choice, all my students made great strides in their use of language. In this chapter, I share some of my most effective lessons.

Ben's writing in January.

Interesting-Word Wall
An Ongoing Display

During Read Aloud and shared reading times, I often stop to comment on interesting words, and I encourage students to do the same. They *ooh* and *ahh* at notable words, such as *admire*, *genuine*, and *trembled*. We talk about how these words are specific and natural, and how they enhance the meaning of the text. I often invite students to put their thumbs up when they hear a word they like. We discuss word meanings and make a mental note of words we want to add to our interesting-word wall. At the end of each reading session, I write a word or two on index cards and we display them on our wall.

Throughout the year, students find words during silent reading and partner book time. They write the words on cards and add these to the wall. As our word bank grows, we discuss the words that have been added. We play word-meaning guessing games, recall the stories from which the words came, and brainstorm synonyms and antonyms for the words. Most importantly, students refer to the word wall for inspiration when they are writing. Our wall lays a foundation for the word-choice lessons that follow in the weeks ahead.

We add words to our interesting-word wall throughout the year.

Word Search
Collecting Powerful Words

Before children begin to use interesting words in their writing, they need to be able to recognize effective word choice in published works. Seeing lots of examples of energetic verbs, specific nouns, and memorable phrases will fill students' minds with language that they can use in their own writing. As a class, study examples of interesting word choice in all kinds of fiction and nonfiction genres—stories, articles, poems, letters, and so on. As you read each piece, invite students to identify and discuss word choice. Invite them to talk about the mental images that the words create. Once students have had opportunities to discuss word choice in pieces you have read together, encourage them to search for powerful words on their own.

One way I do this is with an interesting-word search activity, using clipboards and photocopies of the reproducible on page 103. I have students partner up and take clipboards and several books to a designated spot in the classroom. Together, students look through the books for interesting words. They record these on their sheets and then think of the common word the author could have used instead, for example:

INTERESTING WORD	COMMON WORD
chortled	laughed
raced	ran
slender	thin
exhausted	tired
snatched	took

Once students have filled their pages, I call the class back together to discuss their findings.

Name Lindsey   Date 2/6
Interesting Word Search

Common Word	Interesting Word
yes	eh
said	chirped
walked	waddled
flew	swooped
loud	hissing
really hot	boiling
rough	jagged
not often	rarely
sharp	rugged
falling down	crumbling
explode	erosion
sleeping	slumbering

Name Malcolm   Date 2-5
Interesting Word Search

Common Word	Interesting Word
falls	cascades
Mean	ferocious
shine	shimmer
Pritty	Gorgous
said	murmured
ran	dashed
scared	terrified
stepping	Plodding
tell	demand

Students chart interesting words found in books, as well as common words that could have been used instead.

Students love to share their discoveries. Together, we compare words, discuss the mental pictures created by specific words and phrases, and talk about how authors are strong stewards of their words. Most important, students realize the power of a word or phrase, which motivates them to include interesting words in their own writing.

Follow-Up

To encourage students to search for words in their independent reading, I provide copies of the bookmark on page 104 and ask students to record their findings on the bookmark as they read.

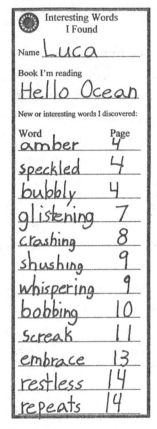

Interesting Words I Found

Name Luca

Book I'm reading

Hello Ocean

New or interesting words I discovered:

Word	Page
amber	4
speckled	4
bubbly	4
glistening	7
crashing	8
shushing	9
whispering	9
bobbing	10
screak	11
embrace	13
restless	14
repeats	14

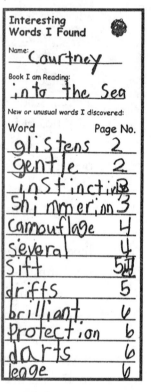

Interesting Words I Found

Name: Courtney

Book I am Reading:

into the Sea

New or unusual words I discovered:

Word	Page No.
glistens	2
gentle	2
instinctive	3
shimmering	3
camouflage	4
several	4
sift	5
drifts	5
brilliant	6
protection	6
darts	6
leage	6

Students record interesting words on bookmarks.

Energetic Verbs
Dramatizing Their Power

Because the right verb can give energy to a piece of writing, verbs are an important focus in my word-choice instruction. To introduce the power of active verbs, I share Denise Fleming's *In the Small, Small Pond*. For this activity, we push the furniture aside to create a large open space in the classroom. After reading the book aloud, I lead a discussion about the pictures, creatures, and actions. We discuss how Fleming's use of specific words lets her relay a lot of information with just a few words.

As I read the book a second time, I ask students to "become" the pond creatures—herons, whirligigs, geese, and dragonflies. (If I'm teaching older students, I often invite a class of younger students to join us. Working with younger students encourages older students to join in the playacting.) As I read, I invite students to dramatize the verbs to show the animals' actions. They *plunge* like herons, *twirl* like whirligigs, and *scatter* like minnows. In the process, students gain a deeper understanding of the power of verbs. As children *wriggle* like tadpoles or *hover* like dragonflies, their movements allow them to capture the meaning of the word. Through this activity, students develop a greater respect for why authors choose the words they do.

After acting out the roles, we make a chart of all the energetic verbs in the book. I display the chart for students to use as reference for any writing activity.

Follow-Up

On another day, we read Fleming's *Where Once There Was a Wood*. Again, we act out energetic verbs and record them on a chart. We repeat this process with several books.

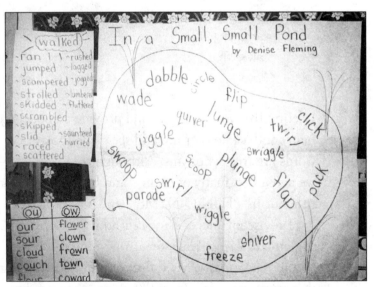

Class chart of verbs from Denise Fleming's **In the Small, Small Pond.**

Fun-o-nyms
Alternatives to Ordinary Words

One of the things I come across year after year is the overuse of certain words—she is *nice*; I had *fun*; it was *good*. In an effort to retire ordinary words and encourage the use of more original ones, I begin a lesson by sharing my own writing about a weekend experience.

This weekend I went to a Mariners baseball game. We had a fun time. We saw four home runs and two stolen bases. The crowd cheered loudly when the center fielder made a great catch. It would have been a home run for the other team but he saved the day. We ate lots of peanuts and popcorn. It was fun.

I then reflect out loud about my piece. "I think I had a clear opening line. I included many details, but the word *fun* isn't very lively. I could use a more interesting word in that place. Can anyone brainstorm some other words that we could use instead of *fun?*"

Students come up with the following list:

brilliant	fascinating
fantastic	incredible
great	terrific
perfect	wonderful
amazing	delightful
awesome	magnificent
lovely	stupendous

I define the word *synonym* and provide some examples of synonyms, such as *funny* and *hilarious* or *ran* and *sped*. We look at our list and discuss whether these words are true synonyms. Although they don't have the exact meaning as *fun*, we agree that many of them could be used to describe things that are fun. We title our list "FUN-O-NYMS," an idea inspired by my colleague, Connie Roepke.

I revise my piece, using *delightful* and *amazing* in place of *fun*. I then ask students to write about something fun they have done recently, such as going to a movie or party. My only requirement: they cannot use the word *fun*. Instead, they must use words from the chart, or find other words. I give students time to share ideas for writing topics and brainstorm alternatives for *fun*.

On subsequent days, students nominate other words to retire, such as *nice*, *said*, and *went*, and we make charts of alternates for these words. I display the charts for students to use as resources for any writing assignment.

Follow-Up

If I notice a student struggling with word choice, I may ask that student to share her paper with the group to help her replace ordinary words. With permission, I make an overhead transparency of the student's paper and ask her to circle two or three words she would like help with. As a group, we suggest alternate words that might liven up the piece. The writer makes the changes when she hears a word that she likes.

I encourage students to ask each other for word help on a regular basis. I remind them that they can be wonderful resources for one another and that good writers often rely on help from other writers to improve their work.

LESSON 19

Word Choice Antics
An Inspiring Alphabet Book

One of my favorite alphabet books is *Antics!* by Cathi Hepworth. On each page the word *ant* is hidden in a longer, more interesting word. A colorful picture illustrates the meaning of the word. For example, the word *flamboyant* appears on the page for *F*, accompanied by an illustration of an elaborately dressed ant. *H* is for *hesitant*, illustrated by a frightened ant standing atop a high diving board. *B* is for *brilliant*. An ant that resembles Albert Einstein is shown working in a chemistry laboratory.

When I share this book with students, we read the word on each page and discuss or predict its meaning, using the picture for clues. Students are delighted with the concept of the book, which is a wonderful resource for words they can use in their writing. We discuss pieces they are working on and the possibility of adding any of these words to them. For example, Richelle is writing about her dog. In her draft, she has written, "My dog is so smart," and has supported that statement with examples. Another student suggests that Richelle change *smart* to *brilliant*. Joey writes about winning a contest. Instead of using the word *excited* to describe how he felt, he decides to use *jubilant*.

Follow-Up

I divide the class into small groups and have each group make their own alphabet book. I encourage students to use powerful words to represent each letter and create illustrations to match the text. We add these books to our class library to reinforce the importance of choosing strong words.

Word Choice: Picture Books for Exploring the Trait

Alphabet Books

Amazon Alphabet by Martin and Tanis Jordan

Antics! by Cathi Hepworth

The Disappearing Alphabet by Richard Wilbur

Quilt Alphabet by Lesa Cline-Ransome

Fiction

Amos & Boris by William Steig

Armadillo Tattletale by Helen Ketteman

Barefoot: Escape on the Underground Railroad by Pamela Duncan Edwards

The Bee Tree by Patricia Polacco

Crickwing by Janell Cannon

Frank and Ernest by Alexandra Day

Giraffes Can't Dance by Giles Andreae

In the Small, Small Pond by Denise Fleming

Raising Sweetness by Diane Stanley

Saving Sweetness by Diane Stanley

Sylvester and the Magic Pebble by William Steig

Time to Sleep by Denise Fleming

When Lightning Comes in a Jar by Patricia Polacco

Nonfiction Books

Appalachia: The Voices of Sleeping Birds by Cynthia Rylant

Cloud Dance by Thomas Locker

Hoops by Robert Burleigh

North Country Night by Daniel San Souci

One Leaf Rides the Wind by Celeste Davidson Mannis

Rainforest by Helen Cowcher

Walk With a Wolf by Janni Howker

Water Dance by Thomas Locker

Where Once There Was a Wood by Denise Fleming

Biography

A Brilliant Streak: The Making of Mark Twain by Kathryn Lasky

Mozart: World-Famous Composer by Diane Cook

Sacagawea by Lise Erdrich

Thank You, Sarah! The Woman Who Saved Thanksgiving
    by Laurie Halse Anderson

Poetry

Beast Feast by Douglas Florian

Dandelions: Stars in the Grass by Mia Posada

Lemonade Sun and Other Summer Poems by Rebecca Kai Dotlich

Sports Pages by Arnold Adoff

Tyrannosaurus Was a Beast by Jack Prelutsky

Under the Sunday Tree by Eloise Greenfield

Books With Energetic Verbs

Barefoot: Escape on the Underground Railroad by Pamela Duncan Edwards

The Bee Tree by Patricia Polacco

Giraffes Can't Dance by Giles Andreae

Look Out, Patrick! by Paul Geraghty

Time to Sleep by Denise Fleming

The Sun, the Wind and the Rain by Lisa Westberg Peters

CHAPTER 5:

Sentence Fluency

CHARACTERISTICS OF THE SENTENCE FLUENCY TRAIT

◎ natural rhythm

◎ fluent phrasing that is music to the ear

◎ sentence constructions that support the content

◎ varied sentence beginnings and length

Adapted from *6+1 Traits of Writing: The Complete Guide, Grades 3 and Up*
by Ruth Culham (Scholastic, 2003).

*"It's fine writing that keeps the audience rapt: it's exquisitely
constructed sentences; it's carefully honed cadences;
it's the marvelous satisfaction of the sensual rhythm of perfect prose."*

— Mem Fox, from
Radical Reflections

Mem Fox says it so eloquently. When we're curled up on the couch with a great
book, what makes us stop mid-page and read aloud a phrase or passage? The
answer has to do with the loveliness of language. As I read Arthur Golden's
Memoirs of a Geisha, I found myself reading aloud many passages. Not only did the
content of those passages speak to me, but so did the beautifully crafted sentences.

Writing expert Ruth Culham (2003) defines fluent writing as "graceful, varied,
rhythmic—almost musical. It's easy to read aloud. Sentences are well built. They
move. They are varied in structure and length. Each one seems to flow right out of
the one before. Strong sentence fluency is marked by logic, creative phrasing,
parallel construction, alliteration, and word order that makes the reading feel natural."

It's fluency that makes us want to share a piece of writing aloud. Well-crafted language begs to be heard. That's why using oral language as a beginning point for young writers is an essential part of teaching students about this trait. Some oral connections are:

◎ teacher reading aloud to students

◎ choral readings as a class

◎ paired readings

◎ Readers Theater

To develop a sense of sentence fluency, students need to participate in oral language activities using strong examples of fiction, poetry, and nonfiction. When students have many experiences hearing smooth, rhythmic language, they are more likely to strive for it in their own work.

As students progress in their writing skills, begin working with them on creating a natural sound by encouraging them to vary their sentence lengths and sentence beginnings. Show them how sentences can be expanded or shortened. Introduce similes, metaphors, and sentence fragments. Demonstrate how to use transitional words and phrases to connect ideas.

I begin teaching students about using sentence fluency in their own writing after they have learned to develop their ideas in an organized manner, and while they are learning about word choice and voice. The following mini-lessons provide some ideas for teaching students how to expand, combine, and manipulate sentences to build a piece of writing that flows naturally.

LESSON 20

Reading Aloud
Hearing the Rhythm and Flow

Reading aloud is the best way to begin teaching sentence fluency. Students need to hear the flow of language, the variety in sentence beginnings and sentence lengths, and the use of connectives that link sentences and ideas. They need to hear fluent language on an ongoing basis in order to write fluently themselves. When you come across a melodic sentence during a Read Aloud, repeat the sentence to give students a chance to internalize it. Ask students to comment on its sound and flow.

I love to read stories aloud while students sit back, relax, and inhale the beautiful language, as in this example from *All the Places to Love* by Patricia MacLachlan:

> *My grandmother loved the river best of all the places to love.*
> *That sound,* like a whisper, *she said;*
> *where trout flashed like jewels in the sunlight.*

The language moves quickly and easily, almost like a river itself. The phrase "of all the places to love" rolls off the tongue. The word *whisper* sounds like its meaning—an example of onomatopoeia.

Another passage I like to share is Roald Dahl's description of the great peach as it breaks free from its branch and begins rolling down the hill in *James and the Giant Peach*:

> *Faster and faster and faster it went, and the crowds of people who were*
> *climbing up the hill suddenly caught sight of this terrible monster*
> *plunging down upon them and they screamed and scattered to right*
> *and left as it went hurtling by.*

Dahl builds a sense of urgency right from the start with the repetition of "Faster and faster and faster." You can't help but read faster; the structure of the sentence perfectly matches the meaning. Dahl uses alliteration with phrases like "suddenly caught sight" and "screamed and scattered." All these techniques make the passage just plain fun to read aloud.

Langston Hughes, Eloise Greenfield, and Karla Kuskin are some of my favorite poets. Sharing poetry aloud is a great way to help students develop a sense of rhythm and cadence. Talk about a poet's repetition of a word or phrase and explain how that adds to a poem's fluency. Revisit books to look for varied sentence beginnings, similes and metaphors, specific descriptions, alliteration, varied sentence lengths, and just simply stunning language that is begging to be read out loud!

This is a good time to begin an ongoing discussion about how the writing traits are intertwined. What techniques does an author or poet use to make the writing more fluent? How is the fluency affected by her word choices and ideas? How does the fluency affect the voice of a piece? Guide students to see that the traits are not isolated characteristics of writing—they overlap and work together to produce the overall effect of a piece.

Remember, you can be working on one trait while emphasizing the others, too. Reading beautiful language aloud simply to hear how it sounds will set the stage for fluent writing. No assignments, no specific tasks—just enjoy!

Excerpts From Books With Notable Sentence Fluency

Expanding With Detail and an Afterthought

"In the winter, when patches of the river froze, Sam and his friends were drawn there to go skating, preferably at night and without permission."

—*A Brilliant Streak: The Making of Mark Twain* by Katherine Lasky

Combining and Expanding Ideas

"Propped on her elbows with her chin in her fists, she stared at the black wolf, trying to catch his eye."

—*Julie of the Wolves* by Jean Craighead George

Varied Sentence Length: Short Followed by Long

"I reined her in quickly. My heels were down, my tail tucked under, the reins light in my fingers—I remembered everything I'd been taught."

—*Mrs. Mack* by Patricia Polacco

Varied Sentence Length: Long Followed by Short

"Down and down and down it came and landed, thunk, on this mountain, sort of cockeyed and shaky and grateful to be all in one piece. Well, sort of one piece."

—*Missing May* by Cynthia Rylant

A List-Like Quality, With a Repeating Structure in Each Phrase, Giving Focus to the Descriptors

(Be careful trying this—E. B. White is a master of making this work.)

"It was the best place to be, thought Wilbur, this warm delicious cellar, with the garrulous geese, the changing seasons, the heat of the sun, the passage of swallows, the nearness of rats, the sameness of sheep, the love of spiders, the smell of manure, and the glory of everything."

—*Charlotte's Web* by E. B. White

Color Poems
Sentence-Building

To help students move from simple sentences to more complex sentences, I start with a controlled exercise called "Color Poems." This activity gives students the opportunity to expand sentences within a specific structure. Once they understand the technique of expanding sentences, I encourage them to apply the same skill to other types of writing.

I begin the mini-lesson by writing "Red" at the top of an overhead transparency. Below it I add the stem *Red looks like . . .* I tell students I want to think of something that reminds me of the color red. I settle on *Red looks like a fire engine.* I write the next line, *Red sounds like . . .* and ask students to help me think of something that seems like a red sound. Ben offers "Red sounds like a crackling fire." We continue with the other senses and end up with the following poem:

Red
Red looks like a fire engine.
Red sounds like a crackling fire.
Red smells like a rose.
Red tastes like red-hot candy.
Red feels like velvet.

We reread the poem. I reflect aloud that the sentences seem short and I think we can add something to each. I read the first sentence again and ask, "Where is the fire engine going?"

Jenny answers, "Zooming down the street." We add this to the poem.

I then read the second line and say, "Tell me more about this fire."

Jason offers, "Red sounds like a crackling fire on a crisp fall evening." We continue through each line and end up with the poem below.

Red looks like a fire engine zooming down the street.
Red sounds like a crackling fire on a crisp fall evening.
Red smells like a beautiful rose in my garden.
Red tastes like red-hot candy burning on my tongue.
Red feels like the velvet on my lovely Christmas dress.

As we compare the two poems, I guide students to notice the difference in the lengths of the sentences. I explain that by adding a detail to each idea, we were expanding our sentences.

I invite students to choose a color and follow the same pattern to write their own poems—a short poem with simple sentences followed by a revised version with longer sentences and more details. As they are writing, I encourage students to help others who are stumped for an idea. For example, while Jason worked on his sentence for "smell," he wanted to think of a flower that was blue. Another child, who had just read about Texas blue bonnets, suggested lupines. I find that, with a little encouragement, students are able to support each other in writing more fluent sentences.

Black

Black sounds like crickets in the night.
Black tastes like Black berries that have just picked.
Black smells like bernt ashes left in the fireplace.
Black feels like Black rabbit fur.
Black looks like Black l'Kireth.

Summer's and Emily's color poems.

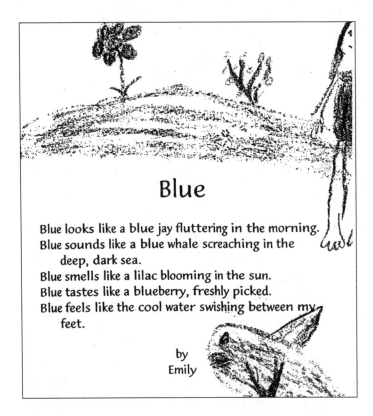

Blue

Blue looks like a blue jay fluttering in the morning.
Blue sounds like a blue whale screaching in the
   deep, dark sea.
Blue smells like a lilac blooming in the sun.
Blue tastes like a blueberry, freshly picked.
Blue feels like the cool water swishing between my
   feet.

by
Emily

Describe a Season
Expanding Sentences

I find that young writers often fall into the pattern of writing stunted sentences, even when they compose longer pieces. (*We went camping. My dad and I set up the tent. Then we went fishing. I like fishing.*) This kind of writing displays little variety in sentence length, structure, or beginnings. As a result, the writing lacks cadence.

The following activity, inspired by my colleagues Mary Ruth Thomas and Cynthia Heffernan, offers an effective way to help students expand choppy sentences and develop sentence fluency. To begin, I create a four-column chart on chart paper, writing the title "Spring" at the top. (It is a good idea to focus the activity on the current season so students may draw from recent observations.) I start by labeling the two center columns: "What Is It?" and "What Can It Do?"

Next I ask students what they see during springtime. Under "What Is It?" I record their responses, such as *birds*, *tulips*, *grass*, *ladybugs*, and *sun*. Then I ask students what each of these "things" are doing and record their responses under "What Can It Do?" Our chart now looks like this:

SPRING

What Is It?	What Can It Do?
birds	sing songs
tulips	bloom
grass	tickles my feet
ladybugs	crawl
sun	shines

Together, we read the text as sentences, moving down our list:

Birds sing songs.
Tulips bloom.
Grass tickles my feet.
Ladybugs crawl.
The sun shines.

I suggest that we expand the sentences by adding more information. To the left, I write the column heading "What Is It Like?" and to the right, I add the column heading "Where Does It Do the Action?" Next, I ask students to describe each of the "things" and record their responses under "What Is It Like?"

Finally, I ask students to tell where the "thing" does the action. To help with this last column, I provide a short list of prepositions, such as *in*, *along*, *on*, *below*, and *by*. I record their responses in the last column to complete the chart.

SPRING

What Is It Like?	What Is It?	What Can It Do?	Where Does It Do the Action?
blue	birds	sing songs	on my windowsill
colorful	tulips	bloom	in my grandmother's garden
cool, green	grass	tickles my feet	as I walk in my yard
spotted	ladybugs	crawl	along my arm
sizzling	sun	shines	on my face

Now we are ready to join these words and phrases together to form sentences. After writing each of the sentences, we work together to add a sentence to introduce the piece and one to wrap it up. I record our finished piece:

Spring
Spring is a wonderful season.
Bluebirds sing songs on my windowsill.
Colorful tulips bloom in my grandmother's garden.
Cool, green grass tickles my feet as I walk in my yard.
Spotted ladybugs crawl along my arm.
The sizzling sun shines on my face.
Spring is fantastic!

Finally, I have students complete their own charts, using the reproducible on page 105. I encourage students to draw inspiration from the class chart and generate their own ideas as well. Once they've completed their charts, students write their "expanded sentences" as final pieces. Some students choose to illustrate their work with watercolor paints, crayons, or colored pencils.

This activity gives students a chance to practice writing fluent sentences so they know what it feels like and what fluent sentences sound like. Focusing on one sentence at a time, rather than a whole piece, leads to student success. Once students are comfortable writing fluent sentences in shorter pieces, they will be better prepared to apply this skill to longer pieces as well.

Follow-Up

Have students complete the Sentence-Building Chart to write about any topic.
Once they've completed the chart, invite them to use the sentences in a piece
about the topic.

Essence of Spring
by Ally

Spring is a beautiful season.
Soft, brown fawns struggle in the meadow.
Loud bees buzz in their hives
Silent ladybugs glide in the air.
Quiet ducklings quack in the pond.
Pretty flowers bloom in the garden.
Slow owls hoot in the night.
Sweet, yellow chicks chirp in their nests.
Big, fluffy trees stand in the forest.
Small puppies lick as they jump on you.
Furry kittens play as they get caught in yarn.
See! Spring is a beautiful season!

Ally's "Essence of Spring" shows her expanded sentences.

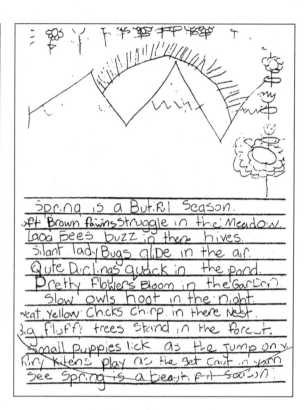

What's it like?	What is it?	What can it do?	Where does it do it?
white	balls	fly	over the field wall
talented	pichers	throw	faster than a car mo
eager	batters	hit	a line drive up first ba line
speedy	players	run like	the wind around the base
hard working	venders	sell popcorn	as they trudge up an down the stairs
excited	fans	cheer	in the stands when their team wins

Name: Jason
Topic: Baseball

Baseball

Baseball is an action-packed sport!
White balls fly over the center-field wall.
Talented pitchers throw faster than a car moves.
Eager batters hit a line drive up the first base line.
Speedy players run like the wind around the bases.
Hard working vendors sell popcorn as they
    trudge up and down the stadium stairs.
Excited fans cheer in the stands
    when their team wins!
Baseball is the All-American sport!

By Jason

Jason completed a chart as a prewriting activity before composing his piece about baseball.

Revising for Sentence Fluency
Expanding and Combining Sentences

Sometimes the most effective way to teach a skill is to show a piece of writing that isn't working. For example, I display the following paragraph on the overhead:

My Kitten

I have a kitten. Her name is Snowball. She is white. She has one black paw. She is furry. She likes to play with yarn. She likes to pull yarn across the room. She makes a mess. Snowball likes to climb trees. Once she got stuck. She couldn't get down. Then she did. Snowball cuddles with me. Snowball got sick once. I took care of her. She got better. I love my kitten.

I read the piece aloud and ask students what they think of it. Most students comment that the piece is boring and that many of the sentences start with the same words. They agree that it didn't flow when it was read out loud. After more discussion, I tell students that what I am hearing from them is that the piece lacks fluency.

I engage students in a revision activity by starting with the question, "How can we improve the fluency of this piece of writing?" Students respond with the following suggestions:

◎ Start sentences with different words.

◎ Combine short sentences.

◎ Add details to sentences.

With these strategies in mind, we begin our "attack" on the sample paragraph, starting with the first two sentences: *I have a kitten. Her name is Snowball.* I ask students, "What questions do you have about this kitten? Remember to use these question words to help you: *Who, What, When, Where, Why,* and *How.*" I post these words for students to refer to.

Ben asks, "What kind of kitten?"

"Is it special?" adds Tyler.

"How did you get the kitten?" asks Jenny.

Then students share ideas for revising the sentence, using the questions to guide them. We come up with: *I found a unique kitten whom I named Snowball.* We then move on to revising the next sentences: *She is white. She has one black paw. She is furry.* Students start asking questions. "Which paw is black?" asks Emily.

Michael wonders, "What kind of fur? Is it thick or smooth or fluffy?"

I ask, "Can we combine these short sentences?" At this time I share combining words such as *and, while, with,* and *as.*

Students share ideas and we decide on the following: *She is white with one black back paw and fur like a thick winter coat.* We continue this process until we end up with the following revision.

> I found a unique kitten whom I named Snowball. She is white with one black back paw and fur like a thick winter coat. Snowball plays 99 percent of the day. Yarn is her toy of choice. She loves to pull it all the way across the room so that it makes a fantastic mess!

Once students feel comfortable with this process, I ask if anyone would like help from the class in revising their pieces for fluency. As a class or in small groups, classmates suggest the same strategies we used on the kitten paragraph to help these volunteers improve the fluency of their pieces.

Follow-Up

◎ Read aloud *Cats* by Gail Gibbons or *Wolves* by Seymour Simon. Talk about the way these authors expand and combine sentences to build a fluent piece of writing.

◎ Make a photocopy of the reproducible on page 106 and write a short starter sentence for students to rewrite. Give students a copy of the page and encourage them to write an expanded sentence that answers the questions on the sheet. To model this activity, I make an overhead transparency of the reproducible and fill it in with students' assistance. Explain that to answer the question "Who or what?" students can add descriptive words about the subject of the sentence. Students can also use this reproducible to revise short sentences in their own writing.

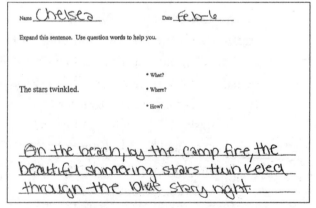

Emma and Chelsea completed the reproducible to expand the sentence "The stars twinkled."

Exploring Similes
One Way to Build Sentence Fluency

I like to read aloud books with similes long before I point them out to students or teach students the definition of a simile. As I've said before, children need lots of wonderful language read to them to prepare them to produce that kind of writing themselves. And, to me, similes make for wonderful language. A well-crafted simile can add cadence to a sentence. If the writer has considered the sounds of the words used, the simile can be delightful to read aloud. It's also an effective way of adding variety to sentence structure.

After I've read aloud a number of similes in books, I formally introduce the term and its meaning. I start by reading *Amber on the Mountain* by Tony Johnston. This book includes several similes, including one in its lead sentence: "Amber lived on a mountain so high, it poked through the clouds like a needle stuck in down." I pause and say, "Hey, the author did something really neat here. She's comparing two things that aren't really alike and telling us how they are alike in one way. Can anyone tell me the two things she's comparing?" I read the sentence aloud a second time.

Cole answers, "The mountain and a needle."

"Yes. How are they alike?" I ask.

"They both poke through something," Teri responds.

"Yeah, one pokes through the clouds and the other pokes through the down pillow," says Taylor.

I answer, "You're right. That's called a simile." I write the word on a chart. I continue reading the next sentence: "Trees bristled on it like porcupine quills." Again, I draw students' attention to the comparison by saying, "Hey, here's another simile. What is the author comparing this time?"

Trevor answers, "Trees and porcupine quills."

Then I ask, "How are they alike?"

The class answers, "They both bristle." I continue reading the book, pausing to point out and discuss similes along the way.

For the next couple of weeks, I read more books with similes. Whenever we come across one during Read Aloud, we stop and talk about it. When the simile is especially lovely, I invite students to repeat the line with me. After reading "where trout flashed like jewels in the sunlight" from Patricia MacLachlan's *All the Places to Love*, I say, "Oh, that's so beautiful. Can anyone else see the colors of the trout in the river? Let's all say this simile together." Students repeat the line with me, and I follow with, "Good authors write such beautiful lines."

To encourage an ongoing awareness of similes, we begin to record on a chart similes that we have come across. Students add to the chart, noting the similes they find on their own. It doesn't take long before we have compiled quite a list.

When I feel students are ready to apply similes to their own writing, I model how to do this. For example, I think aloud as I write a description of my neighbor's dog: "He's really fierce. Maybe I could use a simile here and say he's as fierce as another kind of animal. I know: *He's as fierce as a tiger*." This modeling becomes a stepping stone for students to try using similes in their own writing. Eventually, I notice students suggesting similes to their classmates when they are revising pieces.

Sentence Fluency: Picture Books for Exploring the Trait

Books With Powerful Similes

All the Places to Love by Patricia MacLachlan

Dancing in the Wings by Debbie Allen

The Lion and the Little Red Bird by Elisa Kleven

Night Noises by Mem Fox

Owl Moon by Jane Yolen

Quick as a Cricket by Audrey Wood

Wilfrid Gordon McDonald Partridge by Mem Fox

Fiction

Amber on the Mountain by Tony Johnston

Caleb & Kate by William Steig

Follow the Drinking Gourd by Jeanette Winter

Little Lil and the Swing-Singing Sax by Libba Moore Gray

My Mama Had a Dancing Heart by Libba Moore Gray

A River Dream by Allen Say

The Table Where Rich People Sit by Byrd Baylor

Tar Beach by Faith Ringgold

Nonfiction

The Eyes of Gray Wolf by Jonathan London

Fabulous Frogs by Linda Glaser

Hoops by Robert Burleigh

Mountain Dance by Thomas Locker

North Country Night by Daniel San Souci

Somewhere Today by Bert Kitchen

Stars by Seymour Simon

Walk With a Wolf by Janni Howker

Water Dance by Thomas Locker

Worksong by Gary Paulsen

Biography

A Brilliant Streak: The Making of Mark Twain by Kathryn Lasky

Duke Ellington by Andrea Davis Pinkney

Eleanor by Barbara Cooney

Poetry

Casey at the Bat: A Ballad of the Republic, Sung in the Year 1888
    by Ernest Lawrence Thayer

Harlem by Walter Dean Myers

Honey, I Love and Other Love Poems by Eloise Greenfield

Paul Revere's Ride by Henry Wadsworth Longfellow

Silver Seeds by Paul Paolilli

Under the Quilt of Night by Deborah Hopkinson

Under the Sunday Tree by Eloise Greenfield

CHAPTER 6:

Conventions and Presentation

CHARACTERISTICS OF THE CONVENTIONS TRAIT

◎ correct spelling, capitalization, punctuation, grammar, and usage

◎ effective paragraphing that strengthens the structure of the piece

◎ use of conventions that adds style and supports the reader's understanding of the text

CHARACTERISTICS OF THE PRESENTATION TRAIT

◎ pleasing and accessible appearance

◎ neat handwriting or inviting fonts

◎ uniform margins

◎ page numbers, bullets, headings, and other guides that help readers find information

◎ effective use of visuals, such as illustrations, charts, and graphs

Adapted from *6+1 Traits of Writing: The Complete Guide, Grades 3 and Up* by Ruth Culham (Scholastic, 2003).

"Potations, exponations . . . we're learning so many marks, I can't keep them all straight!"

— Matt, first-grader

The traits can be grouped into two categories: revision traits and editing/publishing traits. The first category includes ideas, organization, voice, word choice, and sentence fluency—all the traits that lend themselves to revising a piece in order to improve the message. The last two traits, conventions and presentation, focus on preparing a piece of writing for an audience.

A few years ago I received from an acquaintance a two-page, single-spaced letter that contained so many spelling, punctuation, and grammatical errors, I had a difficult time focusing on the content. The experience made me realize that while conventions and presentation aren't the most important parts of writing, they do have a valuable role.

Ruth Culham (2003) states that the purpose of conventions "is to guide the reader through text and make ideas readable." Writers use capitalization, punctuation, and paragraphing to tell the reader when a new thought is starting and when one has concluded. They use commas to signal when to pause, perhaps to give emphasis to an idea. Correct spelling and grammar ensure clarity, so the meaning is clear to the reader. Presentation is the icing on the cake. Ruth Culham describes it as "how the writing looks to the reader at its heart." The appearance of a piece can either draw readers in or block them from enjoying the content.

If students do not learn to use conventions effectively, they won't be able to communicate their ideas, leaving their readers confused. Or worse, their readers will become so frustrated that they'll stop reading altogether. Students also need to learn the value of making their work presentable to an audience—and specific ways to accomplish this.

It's important to teach conventions in a fun and motivating way. Introduce topics, such as capitalization or commas, using some of the Read Aloud books listed on pages 90 and 91. Conduct interactive mini-lessons using examples of writing. During these lessons, have students observe firsthand the breakdown of meaning when incorrect conventions are used, and how meaning is restored when proper conventions are employed. Model the decisions you make when using conventions, editing in front of students and asking for their input. Focus on the skills your students are ready for. Give them time to practice editing their own writing, with support from you and their peers. Once students have selected an edited piece for presentation, show them how they can create a final piece that is inviting and accessible to the reader.

The following lessons appear in two groups. The first four lessons are designed to help students learn to apply conventions properly as they draft and edit their work. The last three are intended to show students how to prepare their pieces for presentation.

Daily News
Identifying Conventions of Print

As a teacher of many subjects with not enough time to teach them all, I am constantly trying to find ways to combine lessons. Here's an example. I start the day by inviting students to report news from home or school, as a way of allowing them to share important happenings in their lives. From there, I extend the activity into a writing lesson, focusing on conventions.

As students share their news, I record what they say on a chart or overhead transparency. Our list might look like this:

Jessica went to her cousin's house yesterday.
Joe went camping with his mom and dad over the weekend.
Nate, a new student, has joined our class.

After recording two or three sentences, I ask if anyone notices any letter combinations that make certain sounds. I explain that these letter combinations help us as we spell words. As I call on individual students, I hand them a marker to circle their find.

Brooke comes up first and says, "I notice the *ou* in *house*."

Andrew notices the *-ing* suffix and circles it in the word *camping*.

Nate comes up and says, "There's an *er* in the word *over*."

Students continue to find letter combinations, circling and explaining their significance to the class.

On another day, I ask students to focus on one of the following: capitalization and punctuation, high-frequency words, or root words and suffixes. Sometimes I open up the choices and let students circle anything they notice about conventions.

A great benefit of this activity is that students of all ability levels can "play the game." Like many teachers, I have taught students with special needs and very capable students in the same class. What students notice is a reflection of what they are ready to focus on in their own writing.

This activity also allows me to point out certain conventions I am teaching. For example, while working on contractions, I ask, "Who can find the contraction up here?" I can take a moment to teach about where the apostrophe goes and why. When teaching quotation marks, I record student news as direct quotations. The above news would appear like this:

Jessica said, "I went to my cousin's house yesterday."

Joe said, "I went camping with my mom and dad over the weekend."

Nate said, "I just joined this class."

Then I ask, "Why do we use these marks here?" I use this opportunity to teach where the comma goes when using quotation marks. For spelling, I can point out certain words that students frequently misspell in their writing and ask that they attend to these words when they write or edit. The possibilities for incorporating skills into daily news are endless.

LESSON 26

Copy Editor's Marks
Editing With a System

In order for students to learn about editing, we must teach them common copy editor's marks. I start with marks for capital letters, lowercase letters, periods, spelling, delete, insert, and spacing. I display these marks on a chart and tell students we are going to learn about them so that we have a way of communicating how they edit their work.

I begin with the marks for capital and lowercase letters. I've found this to be such a common area of difficulty for students (for example, not beginning sentences with capital letters, yet using them in the middle of sentences). I share the following short piece of writing on a chart:

> Horses are beautiful animals. They come in many colors: brown, black, white, and even gray. Horses have shiny hair that looks like silk. Some horses have braided manes.

I ask students if they see any problems with capital or lowercase letters. We compare the number of sentences (four) with the number of capital letters (four) and agree that there are no problems. There are no proper names mentioned so we don't need any extra capital letters. Then I show students the following piece:

> horses can do many things. they Can jump and Trot. They can Gallop and run. they canter and carry People around.

When I ask students if this piece contains proper use of capital letters, students agree that there are many errors. One by one, we find letters that need to be capitalized or made lowercase. I invite students to write the appropriate copy editor's mark to show what change is needed. After this lesson, I give students a copy of the Starter List of Copy Editor's Symbols (page 107) and the following paragraph to edit for capital and lowercase letters (page 108).

> bears are interesting Animals. There are many different types, Like the black bear, grizzly bear and sun bear. mama Bears are very Protective of their young. They won't let anyone near Them. bears like to eat berries and fish. They have to store up lots of food Because they hibernate for the winter. I like to read about Bears but i would not want to meet one!

On subsequent days, I provide additional pieces for students to edit (pages 109–110). With each piece, we cover different conventions. I begin each lesson by modeling how to edit a short piece, followed by group editing and individual practice. The repeated practice with copy editor's marks helps students commit these to memory.

ℒ	Take it out.	I'm a good good writer.
∧	Put something in.	good I'm a ∧ writer.
⚲	Put in space.	I'm agood writer. ⚲
⊙	Add a period.	I'm a good writer ⊙
≡	Make this a capital letter.	i'm a good writer. ≡
/	Make this capital letter lowercase.	I'm a Good writer.
sp	Correct this spelling error.	sp I'm a good (writter.)

A starter list of copy editor's symbols from 6+1 Traits of Writing: The Complete Guide, Grades 3 and Up by Ruth Culham (Scholastic, 2003).

Trait-Based Mini-Lessons for Teaching Writing in Grades 2–4
SCHOLASTIC TEACHING RESOURCES

Spelling Cards
Creating Responsible Spellers

I used to give my students a list of spelling words on Monday, have them practice these words Tuesday through Thursday, and then give a test on Friday. Most students did very well on Friday's test. However, even the children who scored 100 percent misspelled the simplest words in their everyday writing. Why?

Students study so they will know the words for the test, not so they will spell them correctly in their writing. They are most concerned with the spelling test score because they believe the teacher is as well.

I realized that if I wanted my students to become better spellers in their writing, I needed to start expecting them to. I began with the words students used most often in their own writing. I adapted various high-frequency word lists to create a list of commonly used words. Using the words on this list, I made a spelling reference card for students and encouraged them to use the cards to check every piece of writing they finished.

To show students how to use the spelling card, I model the process. First I write a short paragraph, purposely misspelling a few words. Here's a recent example:

> Harriet (Tubmen) *sp* was a famous American. She saved a lot of slaves on the Underground (Ralroad), (wich) *sp* *sp* was pretty brave because she (coold) *sp* have been caught at any time and taken back to slavery herself.

I tell students that Mrs. Roepke, the teacher in the classroom next door, helped me edit my piece so I would know which words to fix for spelling. "Notice the circles around some words with the letters *sp*. That means I misspelled that word. It might be a word from my spelling card, or it might be a 'topical' word, meaning a word from our topic of study that is on our list in the room.

"Let me begin by getting out my spelling word card. Let's see—can anyone help me figure out what's wrong with this first word?"

Emma says, "I think you didn't spell *Tubman* right. On our list it has an *a* in it, not an *e*."

"Oh, I see that. Let me change that now." I correct the word *Tubman*.

I continue, "How about this next line? I have three misspelled words."

Riley says, "Well, *railroad* isn't right. You need an *ai* in it, not just an *a*."

"Okay, I'll fix that now," I respond.

The students think a bit before Nick notices, "I think *which* has *wh* at the beginning."

"Let me look that up on my card. Yes, you're right." I say. "Way to go, Nick." I make the change. "Now, one more. I think I know this one. It's *c-o-u-l-d*. I just went too quick there." I change *coold* to *could*.

At this point, I ask students to take out their writing folders and select a piece that they would like to edit for spelling. Either by themselves or with a partner, students edit their work, referring to their spelling cards. Afterward, we come back together and students discuss their editing experiences.

Whenever students write, I stress the importance of editing their work and using their spelling word card and any topical lists around the room. I explain to students that these are the words they should be spelling correctly in their writing before they turn it in. I encourage students to ask classmates to check each other's writing for spelling errors as well.

One of my greatest joys in teaching conventions came shortly after I had introduced peer editing to students. In the middle of Writing Workshop I heard one student, Hanna, asking another student, Serena, if she would edit her work. Serena not only agreed but also asked, "What would you like me to edit for—punctuation, spelling, or capitalization?"

Hanna replied, "Spelling, please." Serena took out her spelling card and began to edit.

LESSON 28

Peer Editing
Looking for Capitals and Periods

No matter how much I worked with students on starting sentences with capital letters and ending them with periods (or other end marks), it was never enough. I modeled. Students practiced. I reminded, often several times, right before students began a writing task. Still, as I moved through the room, I found many students beginning sentences with lowercase letters.

This continued until I started using the following lesson. I begin by writing a short piece on chart paper, intentionally including errors in capitalization and punctuation. For example:

yesterday I went to dinner with my friend toni We went to a little restaurant that serves excellent food. She had spaghetti and I had fettuccini. we caught up about what we had been doing over the last few weeks After dinner, we went for a walk We walked all around the lake. next we got ice cream. It was a perfect evening

I read the piece to students and ask, "What do you think of my writing?"

T. J. answers, "You forgot to start some sentences with capital letters."

Cole adds, "And you forgot some periods."

I prod, "Tell me more. Show me where I need a capital letter." T. J. points to the beginning of my first sentence. "Why do I need a capital letter there?"

"Because it starts your sentence," says T. J.

"Oh, that's right. We know we have to begin all sentences with a capital letter. Can anyone find another sentence that needs a capital letter at the beginning?" Two other students come up and point out places where I need to edit for capital letters.

Then Soren says, "I see another place where you need a capital. You have the name *Toni* in your writing."

"Yes, I see that. Why does *Toni* need to have a capital?"

"Because it's the name of a person," states Jessica.

"You're right. Remember, names of places and people have to start with capital letters, too."

Then I direct a question back to Cole. "You said I was missing some periods. Can you show me where I need to put a period and tell me why?"

Cole points out the end of one of my sentences. "You need one here because it's the end of your sentence."

"You reminded me that we always end sentences with an end mark, like a period." I invite a few more students to come up and point out where I missed putting periods and we edit my piece.

After editing my writing, I remind students that we should have at least one capital letter and one end mark for each sentence. We count the sentences and record this number. Then we count and record the number of capital letters and periods, making sure the totals match. We find that we have one additional capital letter and review why we capitalized that word: It's a proper noun, the name of my friend.

I invite students to choose a piece of writing from their writing folders to edit for capitalization and end marks. Afterward, each student pairs up with a classmate and completes the partner editing worksheet that appears on page 111. To complete the form, students count the number of sentences, capital letters, and end marks. If the totals don't match, students check their work for proper nouns, abbreviations, and so on. This extra checking often allows them to catch other errors as well.

Menus, Brochures, and Other "Real-Life" Samples
Studying Visual Elements

The purpose of most of the writing in my classroom centers on the process: on thinking, forming and expressing ideas, and practicing skills. Because of this, my students do not publish all their pieces. However, when students are ready to share their writing publicly, I introduce some key elements of presentation. The purpose of this and other presentation mini-lessons is for students to consider the form of their writing and understand the visual elements that will make their pieces engaging and easy to read.

I begin by sharing various writing samples, both strong and weak in presentation. These include advertisements, menus, brochures, flyers, opening pages from stories, and anonymous handwritten and typed pieces from former students. I divide students into groups and give each group a selection of texts. I ask them to read the samples, noticing which elements—such as font style, font size, spacing, or anything else—engage or distract them as readers. I remind students to consider the purpose of each piece of writing. Why did the writer publish this piece? I have the groups take notes in preparation for sharing their observations with the whole class.

As I walk around the room, I listen to students' discussions. Jason's group is studying two menus. He begins by saying, "This menu's writing is too small. I can hardly read what it says."

Malcolm adds, "Yeah, it would be better if the writing was bigger. I think some people might not take the time to read it all."

"Or maybe if there was more space between each food listed," says Serena.

Jason holds up the other menu and says, "I like this one better. It has a big title at the top that says *Lunch* so you know you have the right menu, and then the food is numbered and the print is big enough to see."

Lisa adds, "And the main items, like *Chicken Sandwich*, are in bold print, and then it explains what is on the sandwich in little plain print underneath."

I ask the group, "Why is that an example of good presentation?"

Lisa answers, "Because you want to be able to look down the menu quickly and see the main items. Then, if you are interested in ordering something, you can look at the smaller print underneath to see if you really want it."

Malcolm adds, "The big, bold print helps the food items stick out."

"Is that what you think the writer of the menu wants?" I ask.

The students nod in agreement. Serena adds, "And the numbers help if you just want to say, 'I'll have a number seven.'"

I move to another group and catch them in the middle of their conversation about a zoo brochure and a flyer for baseball sign-ups. I ask what the group thinks about the flyer. "I like it," says Jordan. "I like baseball."

"As a reader, how do you like the flyer? Is it easy or hard to read?"

Jordan answers, "It's pretty easy to read."

"Why?" I ask.

Claire says, "It has big letters at the top and they're in bold print, so that part gets your attention."

"And then the time and place and everything else is underneath in smaller print, but not too small," adds Jordan.

"Yes. How about this part?" I point to the wide margins where the time, place, and date are listed.

"There's more space on the sides," says Claire.

"Does that help you as a reader or not?" I ask.

Claire responds, "It kind of draws my eyes to that information."

I nod and say, "Sometimes people add a wider margin in places to draw your attention to a certain spot. It can be a good technique as long as all the items are indented to the same spot. You wouldn't want the date to start here and the time to start here." I point to different places on the page. "Otherwise, your eyes would be skipping around trying to find all the information."

I turn to the brochure and ask students to sum up what they found. Emma begins, "Well, we like the picture on the front. It's very colorful. The writing is pretty small but you still notice it. *Woodland Park Zoo* still sticks out even though it's little."

Jenna adds, "And then the word *membership* is in different lettering and it's lighter."

I ask, "Why do you think the author decided to use a picture of a bird for most of the front cover?"

Ben answers, "Because it's a brochure for the zoo and the picture of the bird gets your attention."

"How about the inside?" I ask.

Ben continues, "There's bold print for each kind of membership and then underneath in plain print there's an explanation. There's space between each one but not too much space."

I ask, "Is it easy to read?"

Jenna answers, "Yes."

After students have discussed their samples, we gather together and groups present their findings. I make a T-chart and label one side "Strong Presentation" and the other side "Weak Presentation." Students share the samples, identifying strong and weak points in presentation, as I record their observations on the appropriate sides of the chart. This chart serves as a reference as we embark on other presentation lessons during the next few weeks.

LESSON 30

The Essay
Scoring Texts for Presentation

O nce students have had a chance to observe and discuss presentation techniques in a variety of text forms, we turn our focus to the presentation of handwritten or typed essays. This is the form students will use most often in their school years ahead, so I want them to be confident in preparing finished pieces in this format.

I begin by sharing two or three anonymous writing samples by former students, some handwritten and some typed. Using our chart from the previous lesson, we briefly discuss the strong and weak points of each piece.

Then I give each student a copy of a scoring guide for presentation (page 112) based on the scoring guides that appear in 6+1 *Traits of Writing: The Complete Guide, Grades 3 and Up* by Ruth Culham (Scholastic, 2003). We read through the five attributes listed. I explain that each one has descriptors, which lead to a score of 5, 3, or 1. Viewing the sample pieces through this lens, we will score each piece.

I invite the group to look back at the first handwritten writing sample and then turn to the top of the scoring guide. "Let's look at the first descriptor. What do you think? Is this easy to read? Are the letters clearly formed and are there spaces between words?"

May responds, "Kind of. But I think it is more like the descriptor for a 3 because most of it is pretty neat, but parts of it are harder to read."

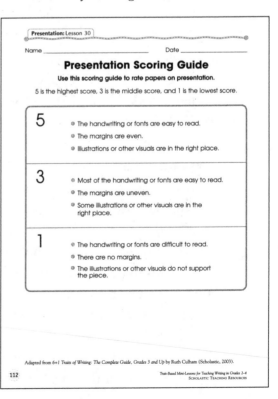

Presentation: Lesson 30

Name _____   Date _____

Presentation Scoring Guide
Use this scoring guide to rate papers on presentation.
5 is the highest score, 3 is the middle score, and 1 is the lowest score.

5
- The handwriting or fonts are easy to read.
- The margins are even.
- Illustrations or other visuals are in the right place.

3
- Most of the handwriting or fonts are easy to read.
- The margins are uneven.
- Some illustrations or other visuals are in the right place.

1
- The handwriting or fonts are difficult to read.
- There are no margins.
- The illustrations or other visuals do not support the piece.

Adapted from 6+1 *Traits of Writing: The Complete Guide, Grades 3 and Up* by Ruth Culham (Scholastic, 2003).
112   *Trait-Based Mini-Lessons for Teaching Writing in Grades 2–4*
SCHOLASTIC TEACHING RESOURCES

I ask, "Does everyone agree?" Students nod. "So for neatness of writing we give the paper a 3. Now, how about the margins? Are the margins even on both sides? Remember, the margins are the white space."

Michael chimes in, "Well, the left side is pretty much the same. There's about an inch all the way down. But on the right side, the writing goes all the way to the edge of the paper."

"Okay," I say. "Let's look at the guide. A 5 means the margins are even. A 3 means the paper has uneven margins."

"It's a 3," a few students say together.

I continue, "The last descriptor is for illustrations, charts, maps, tables, and other visual aids. Since this paper has none of these, we can skip that. So we have a 3 for handwriting neatness and a 3 for margins. That makes it easy to give an overall score."

Emma says, "It's a 3."

We score two other papers for presentation, using the same guide. I then ask students to review one of their own published papers, using the presentation guide. I encourage students to work in pairs, celebrating their presentation strengths and identifying ways they might improve the overall appearance of their pieces.

LESSON 31

Bookmaking
Presenting Fiction and Nonfiction

Students love to present their stories and nonfiction pieces in book format. Before assigning a book project, I get them thinking about design elements by sharing several picture books that represent a variety of genres: fiction, nonfiction, biography, and others. As we discuss the authors' layout of text and illustration, students share their observations. Some responses include:

"Sometimes, like in Seymour Simon's books, there's writing on one side of the page and an illustration on the facing page."

"This book has writing at the bottom and an illustration above."

"The text and the illustration go together."

"Yeah, the writing and the picture match."

"Some longer books only have pictures every few pages."

I share my own thoughts by saying, "Wow, authors really have to think about how they want their books to look. Do you suppose they just start right in, or do you think they make a plan for how much text will go on each page?"

Students agree that authors must make a plan. I then ask, "How do you think an author and illustrator decide on the picture for each page?"

Students agree that the authors and illustrators probably decide what the most important part of the writing is, and then make a picture to match.

I allow more time for students to peruse books, talking with partners about text and illustration layout.

Then I give students their presentation assignment. I ask them to choose an edited piece from their writing folders, either fiction or nonfiction, that they would like to present in book format. Their first task is to think about what kind of text and illustration layout they would like to use. Then they must consider the length of their piece. Finally, they need to determine which parts of their piece are the most important and how they will illustrate these parts.

I ask students to use colored pencils to draw boxes around the text for each page. Then I have them highlight the parts of the text that they will illustrate. Before students begin creating their books, I give them time to review their plans in small groups.

Once students have discussed their plans, received feedback, and made any changes, they are ready to begin. I recall our previous discussions about font size and style, headings, margins, and so on. I remind students of the samples we looked at and how the authors and illustrators integrated the text and illustrations on each page.

For this assignment, students either handwrite or type the text for each page. They determine the layout of each page, draw illustrations, and decide how they will bind their books. This is an ongoing process that students work on over a few weeks. Once they have finished, we share the books with other classes and create a special display in our classroom library.

Conventions and Presentation:
Picture Books for Exploring the Traits

Conventions

The Amazing Pop-Up Grammar Book by Jennie Maizels and Kate Petty

Behind the Mask: A Book About Prepositions by Ruth Heller

A Cache of Jewels and Other Collective Nouns by Ruth Heller

Fantastic! Wow! And Unreal! A Book About Interjections and Conjunctions by Ruth Heller

Grammar Tales: The Bug Book by Maria Fleming

Grammar Tales: Chicken in the City by Maria Fleming

Grammar Tales: Francine Fribble, Proofreading Policewoman
by Justin McCory Martin

Grammar Tales: The Mega-Deluxe Capitalization Machine by Justin McCory Martin

Grammar Tales: The Mystery of the Missing Socks by Justin McCory Martin

Grammar Tales: The No-Good, Rotten, Run-On Sentence by Liza Charlesworth

Grammar Tales: The Planet Without Pronouns by Justin McCory Martin

Grammar Tales: Tillie's Tuba by Maria Fleming

Grammar Tales: A Verb for Herb by Maria Fleming

Grammar Tales: When Comma Came to Town by Samantha Berger

Kites Sail High: A Book About Verbs by Ruth Heller

Many Luscious Lollipops: A Book About Adjectives by Ruth Heller

Merry-Go-Round: A Book About Nouns by Ruth Heller

Mine, All Mine: A Book About Pronouns by Ruth Heller

Punctuation Takes a Vacation by Robin Pulver

Ring! Yo? by Chris Raschka

Up, Up, and Away: A Book About Adverbs by Ruth Heller

The War Between the Vowels and the Consonants by Priscilla Turner

Yo! Yes? by Chris Raschka

Presentation

Chickens Aren't the Only Ones by Ruth Heller

Click, Clack, Moo: Cows That Type by Doreen Cronin

Come On, Rain by Karen Hesse

Giving Thanks: The 1621 Harvest Festival by Kate Waters

How Are You Peeling? by Saxton Freymann and Joost Elffers

In the Small, Small Pond by Denise Fleming

Possum Magic by Mem Fox

Red-Eyed Tree Frog by Joy Cowley

The Three Pigs by David Wiesner

The True Story of the 3 Little Pigs by Jon Scieszka

Wemberly Worried by Kevin Henkes

The Whales by Cynthia Rylant

CHAPTER 7:

Assessment

"The key to assessment is the word itself.
It comes from the Latin verb assidere: *to sit beside.*
We are not ranking here. We are sitting beside a piece of writing and
observing its qualities. We are finding a common language
to talk about those qualities."

— Barry Lane, from
"Quality in Writing"

Of course, when we teach writing, we must also assess it. It is through assessment that we are able to share feedback with students, helping them celebrate their successes, as well as prodding them to improve the skills that need work. Assessment also plays another significant role. It helps us craft future lessons that build on what students know and direct them toward the next steps.

The writing traits model breaks down writing into characteristics so that each one can be discussed and assessed. When the traits are well defined for students, they will have a clear sense of what they are aiming for in their writing. And, once students have finished a piece, they can use the traits to analyze its strengths and weaknesses.

Writing assessment can take many forms. I believe that teachers need to involve students in their assessments. First, it is essential to communicate "the target." What is it students should be aiming for? Make sure the skill you are working on—whether it is a clear lead sentence, specific word choices, or a main topic with supporting details—is communicated to students, modeled, and practiced before they are ever formally assessed.

This chapter provides a snapshot of several types of assessment that I use in my classroom: self-assessment, portfolio assessment, peer assessment, and teacher anecdotal notes. Several assessment reproducibles are provided in the appendix.

Self-Assessment

I believe in engaging students in lots of informal assessments. One way I work with students to co-assess their work is through writing conferences. At these conferences, we look at a student's recent writing and have a conversation about it. We both talk. We both ask questions and make suggestions. I commend the student's successes and ask questions about anything that is unclear or missing.

To prepare for conferences, I have students assess their work using short checklists that I create to focus on what we have been studying. (Self-assessment checklists appear on pages 113–114.) When our focus is on organization, the checklist will include statements such as "Includes a clear beginning, middle, and end" or "Includes a lead sentence, middle sentences with details, and an end sentence." If I have been teaching about expanded sentences, I may ask students to identify a sentence they worked to expand. As we focus on word choice, I ask students to note interesting words they used.

Teacher and student discussing a recent piece at a writing conference.

Name Jessica   Date 6-5

Title: My Beach Feld Trip

☑ I included a lead sentence.

☑ I have middle sentences that include details.

☑ I have an ending sentence.

Here is an interesting word I used: fragel

Jessica's completed checklist for her piece "My Beach Field Trip."

Portfolio Assessment and Reflection

Having students self-evaluate is of paramount importance. I often have students do this through portfolio self-reflections. Once a month, I ask students to look through their writing folders and choose a piece for their writing portfolios. I then have them write a response about this specific piece, identifying its strengths in terms of one or more of the writing traits. Students may also take this opportunity to describe how their writing has changed and improved. The self-reflection sheet (page 115) is attached to the piece and both are added to the writing portfolio.

Sarah reads through the pieces in her writing folder before choosing one for her portfolio.

Name _Summer_   Date _3/31_

❖❖ **SELECTION FOR MY PORTFOLIO** ❖❖

I chose this piece for my portfolio because, I used good word choice. I like huveredeshy

I think you had voice too

Name _Connor_   Date _11-8_

❖❖ **SELECTION FOR MY PORTFOLIO** ❖❖

I chose this piece for my portfolio because
I yousd someny intesting wrds and it was such a chalig To rite. and it was the lagist Story I have ever ritin in my life here is award I yousd.~retret

Students reflect on pieces they have chosen for their portfolios.

Peer Assessment

Peer assessment also plays an important role in my classroom. Buddy checklists or informal sharing groups can often catapult a part of a student's writing to a new level. (A partner checklist appears on page 116.) I encourage students to begin their feedback by identifying a "shining moment" in the piece. What was done well? Once students have identified a strength, I encourage them to move on to how the author might improve the piece.

Students fill in a revision checklist as part of their peer assessment.

> **Revision Checklist**
>
> Name __carol__ Date __4-27__
>
> Title __All the Places to love__
>
> **Self Check:**
>
> ☑ I have read my writing to myself.
>
> ☑ I made at least one change.
>
> My change was made for this trait: __ideas__
>
> Comments: __I think that I had a good voice.__
>
> **Partner Check:**
>
> ☑ I told the writer what I liked.
>
> ☑ I asked questions.
>
> I suggested this change: __a period__ *writing trait*
>
> Comments: __I liked that She used an intristin word chois__
>
> Revising Partner: __Katie__

Teacher Anecdotal Notes

Most of the feedback I provide is verbal, during conferences, but I also like to write short responses to students on sticky notes. General comments such as "Good job!" or "Nice work!" do not give students enough information. Instead, I write comments like, "You included a great lead sentence. It really made me want to read on. Please work on adding an ending sentence." Or, "You used strong word choices like *massive* and *fierce*." If we want students to learn from evaluations, we must be specific.

I place these sticky notes directly on students' work and record the

A sample from my notebook in which I record anecdotal notes about students' writing through the year.

> Anecdotal Notes for __Daesha__
>
> | 9-26 "A Family of Mice" Book -great illustrations developing story | 10-19 "Fall" -included first + last sentences details | 11-6- "Henry-Turkey Story" *Word Choice- "discouraged" "furious" *Beg., mid (problem) |
> | --- | --- | --- |
> | 12-1 Horse Story set up w/characters | 12-14 →experimenting w/ conversation +W.C. "mumbled" | 1-9 "Winter" good lead + end sentence Using periods Work on details |
> | 1-31 "Snakes"- lots of details Revising for W. Choice | 2-17 *Conventions Included simile "rough as sandpaper" Working on sent. expansion | 3-4 "Turtles" many details" Sentences are flowing. Good lead/end. |
> | 4-5 Poems "Trees" adding commas, lots of comparisons. lovely illus. Sense of "whole" | | |

Trait-Based Mini-Lessons for Teaching Writing in Grades 2–4
SCHOLASTIC TEACHING RESOURCES

95

comments in a notebook I use during Writing Workshop. My notebook becomes a continuous record of each student's growth over time. While conferring with students, I record comments specific to the writing traits. These anecdotal notes provide information for the student, parent, and me.

My response to a student's book about spring.

Classroom Assessment vs. Large-Scale Assessment

Of course, all teachers need to assess formally. Our state provides a scoring guide for writing that is used at fourth, seventh, and tenth grades. It is a holistic assessment that includes elements of the first six writing traits and evaluates students on the content and mechanics of their writing. Many school districts create their own scoring guides that are used to evaluate papers at districtwide writing assessments. These scoring guides can be very helpful in providing teachers with specific targets. I often pull apart a scoring guide to use it as a teaching tool. For example, I'll choose one line, such as "includes ample details," and focus my lessons on that goal. I'll create checklists or scoring guides that may include just one item. When I feel students are ready for a new challenge, I'll add another item. And so it goes.

My student teacher, Darlene Moe, created a similar scoring guide that focused on the writing traits students had been working on. Before students began an assignment, she gave them the scoring guide so they would be clear about their targets. Darlene evaluated the finished pieces using her scoring guide and gave students the opportunity to improve their scores. If a student attempted revision, his or her effort score automatically went up by one point. They were able to improve other scores as well. Students responded very positively to this feedback and were eager to revise their writing. (An adapted version of Darlene's scoring guide appears on page 117. Other assessment rubrics appear on pages 118–119.)

Darlene Moe's scoring guide.

Sometimes assessment can be as simple as a small reward. My colleague Cynthia Heffernan and I create award certificates to attach to writing when we see something special. These awards celebrate the use of details, interesting words, voice, and so on. Create your own awards that focus on your goals for students.

Assessment is an essential part of the learning process. Ongoing feedback—written and verbal, formal and informal—is key to students' continued growth as writers. Effective assessment not only motivates students to improve their writing, but it also motivates teachers to focus our teaching. Assessment is a valuable tool—one that can be used to build students' confidence, improve their skills, and inform our teaching.

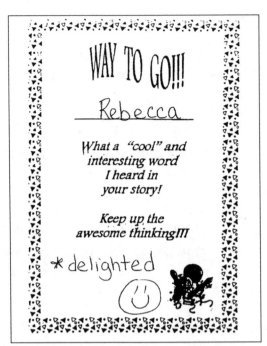

An "Interesting-Word Award" given to a student for using the word delighted.

Final Thoughts

I set out to write this book as a way of sharing with other teachers what I've learned about teaching writing. Focusing on the traits of writing—ideas, organization, voice, word choice, sentence fluency, conventions, and presentation—has helped me craft lessons that I use every day.

When we intentionally teach a trait, model its importance, and allow ample practice time, students begin to write more effectively. Giving students a scheduled time to write every day—beginning with a short mini-lesson on a specific trait, followed by time for drafting and conferring, and ending with a session of sharing and reflecting—is important. Choice in writing is key, as well as involving students in assessing their work.

My hope is that you will take these lessons and make them your own. Begin with one trait and when you feel students are ready, add another trait to your lessons. Take the lead from your students. What are they ready for next? Find books that both you and your students are excited about and use them as models for teaching the traits. Model your own writing for kids as well. Involve students in interactive lessons on revising and editing. Most of all, enjoy the process, and you will teach your students to love writing.

Be specific in your feedback to students. Here are some examples of comments for each trait:

Ideas

"I felt like I was at the ocean because of your detailed description."

"I can really picture your grandmother's face when she was surprised by all of you at her party. You described her with such detail."

Organization

"Your piece started out with a great lead. It made me want to read on."

"You have a clear beginning, middle, and ending, and you paced your story very well—just the right amount of time in each place."

Voice

"I nearly believed your leprechaun was real!"

"You wrote with a clear sense of purpose and audience."

Word Choice

"I love all your descriptive language. *Exquisite*—What a great word to describe the ring."

"Your word choices helped me see exactly how the lion moved."

Sentence Fluency

"Your sentences flow smoothly."

"I like that you started your sentences differently and you varied your sentence lengths."

Conventions

"Good for you! You remembered to use capitals to start all your sentences."

"It is clear that you used your spelling card to spell all your 'no excuse' words."

Presentation

"Your handwriting invites me to read the piece."

"The illustrations and text really work together."

Appendices

APPENDIX A: *Reproducibles for Lessons*

APPENDIX B: *Assessment Reproducibles*

Name _____   Date _____

You're in the Picture

Choose an illustration in the book. List what you see, hear, smell, taste, and feel. On a separate sheet of paper, write a description using the information from your lists.

Book Title:

_____

Author:

_____

I see . . .

_____

_____

_____

_____

I hear . . .

_____

_____

_____

_____

I smell . . .

_____

_____

_____

_____

I taste . . .

_____

_____

_____

I feel . . .

_____

_____

_____

Name _____   Date _____

Showing Sentences

> Good writers use their words to show rather than tell.

Can you turn this telling sentence into a showing sentence or paragraph?

Telling Sentence:

_____

_____

Showing Sentence or Paragraph:

_____

_____

_____

_____

_____

_____

_____

Name _____   Date _____

Voice Scoring Guide

Use this scoring guide to rate papers on voice.

5 is the highest score, 3 is the middle score, and 1 is the lowest score.

5	**The writer . . .** ◎ speaks directly to the reader. ◎ shows himself or herself throughout the piece. ◎ shows that he or she cares about the topic.
3	**The writer . . .** ◎ speaks directly to the reader in a few places. ◎ shows himself or herself in a few places. ◎ seems to care about the topic in a few places.
1	**The writer . . .** ◎ does not connect with the reader. ◎ does not show himself or herself. ◎ does not seem to care about the topic.

Adapted from *6+1 Traits of Writing: The Complete Guide, Grades 3 and Up* by Ruth Culham (Scholastic, 2003).

Name _____   Date _____

Interesting-Word Search

Look for interesting words in your book. Record them in the left column. Then write common words with the same meaning in the right column.

Interesting Word	Common Word
_____	_____
_____	_____
_____	_____
_____	_____
_____	_____
_____	_____
_____	_____
_____	_____
_____	_____
_____	_____
_____	_____
_____	_____

Word Search Bookmark

Name

_____

Book

_____

Author

_____

INTERESTING WORDS I FOUND:

Word   Page

_____

_____

_____

_____

_____

_____

_____

_____

Name

_____

Book

_____

Author

_____

INTERESTING WORDS I FOUND:

Word   Page

_____

_____

_____

_____

_____

_____

_____

_____

Trait-Based Mini-Lessons for Teaching Writing in Grades 2–4
SCHOLASTIC TEACHING RESOURCES

Name _____

Date _____

Sentence-Building Chart

Choose a topic. List your responses to each question below.

Topic: _____

What is it?	What can it do?	Where does it do the action?	What's it like?

Name _____   Date _____

Expanding Sentences

Answer the questions below. Then expand the starter sentence.

Starter Sentence:

_____

_____

◎ Who or what?   _____

_____

_____

◎ Where?   _____

_____

_____

◎ How?   _____

_____

_____

Expanded Sentence:

_____

_____

_____

Trait-Based Mini-Lessons for Teaching Writing in Grades 2–4
SCHOLASTIC TEACHING RESOURCES

A Starter List of Copy Editor's Symbols

℘	Take it out.	I'm a good ~~good~~ writer.
∧	Put something in.	good I'm a ∧ writer.
⟨#⟩	Put in space.	I'm a good writer. ⟨#⟩
⊙	Add a period.	I'm a good writer⊙
≡	Make this a capital letter.	i'm a good writer. ≡
/	Make this capital letter lowercase.	I'm a /Good writer.
sp	Correct this spelling error.	sp I'm a good (writter.)

From 6+1 *Traits of Writing: The Complete Guide, Grades 3 and Up* by Ruth Culham (Scholastic, 2003).

Name _____   Date _____

Editing Practice: Capitalization

Use copy editor's symbols to correct the capitalization errors.

bears are interesting Animals. There are

many different types, Like the black bear,

grizzly bear, and sun bear. mama Bears

are very Protective of their young. They

won't let anyone near Them. bears like to

eat berries and fish. They have to store up

lots of food Because they hibernate for

the winter. I like to read about Bears but i

would not want to meet one!

Trait-Based Mini-Lessons for Teaching Writing in Grades 2–4
SCHOLASTIC TEACHING RESOURCES

Name _____   Date _____

Editing Practice: Spelling

Use copy editor's symbols to correct the spelling errors.

Cats are my favorite animal in the hole
world. Thay like to snuggle with you and
rub up against your legs. Cats lick to curl
up on your lap and take a nap. Whut do
you think a cat's favorite food is? I'm not
sure. I just no my cat loves tuna! I wish I
coud have a house full of cats!

Name _____   Date _____

Editing Practice: Punctuation

Use copy editor's symbols to correct the punctuation errors.

Have you ever considered getting a bird

for a pet. They are fun animals to own

Some can talk Some can sing and some

just make funny sounds. Birds come in

different colors, like yellow blue and red.

They can keep you company when youre

lonely. Isnt that a good enough reason to

want a bird.

Name _____   Date _____

Partner Editing Worksheet

Author: _____   Editor: _____

Topic: _____

_____ I read my partner's writing.

Number of sentences   _____

Number of capitals   _____

Number of end marks   _____

Did the numbers match?   yes   no

If not, which extra words were capitalized?

_____

_____

_____

_____

Did the author use periods in abbreviations? What were they?

_____

_____

_____

_____

Name _____   Date _____

Presentation Scoring Guide

Use this scoring guide to rate papers on presentation.

5 is the highest score, 3 is the middle score, and 1 is the lowest score.

5

◎ The handwriting or fonts are easy to read.

◎ The margins are even.

◎ Illustrations or other visuals are in the right place.

3

◎ Most of the handwriting or fonts are easy to read.

◎ The margins are uneven.

◎ Some illustrations or other visuals are in the right place.

1

◎ The handwriting or fonts are difficult to read.

◎ There are no margins.

◎ The illustrations or other visuals do not support the piece.

Adapted from *6+1 Traits of Writing: The Complete Guide, Grades 3 and Up* by Ruth Culham (Scholastic, 2003).

Name _____   Date _____

Self-Assessment Checklist:
Paragraph Writing

Title: _____

_____   I included a lead sentence.

_____   I included middle sentences with details.

_____   I included an ending sentence.

Here is an interesting word or phrase from my piece:

_____

_____

_____

- -

Name _____   Date _____

Self-Assessment Checklist:
Paragraph Writing

Title: _____

_____   I included a lead sentence.

_____   I included middle sentences with details.

_____   I included an ending sentence.

Here is an interesting word or phrase from my piece:

_____

_____

_____

Name _____ Date _____

Self-Assessment Checklist: Story Writing

Title: _____

_____ My story has a lead sentence.

_____ My story has a problem.

_____ My story has a solution to the problem.

_____ My story has a strong ending sentence.

Here is an interesting word or phrase from my piece:

_____

_____

- -

Name _____ Date _____

Self-Assessment Checklist: Story Writing

Title: _____

_____ My story has a lead sentence.

_____ My story has a problem.

_____ My story has a solution to the problem.

_____ My story has a strong ending sentence.

Here is an interesting word or phrase from my piece:

_____

_____

Name _____   Date _____

Portfolio Self-Reflection

Title: _____

I chose this piece for my portfolio because

_____

_____

_____

_____

_____

- -

Name _____   Date _____

Portfolio Self-Reflection

Title: _____

I chose this piece for my portfolio because

_____

_____

_____

_____

_____

Partner Revision Checklist

Writer: _____

Partner: _____

Title: _____

Self-Check:

_____ I have read my writing to myself.

_____ I made at least one change.

I made a change for this trait: _____

The change I made was _____

_____

Comments: _____

_____

Partner Check:

_____ I told the writer what I liked.

_____ I asked questions.

I suggested a change for this trait: _____

The change I suggested was _____

_____

Comments: _____

_____

Name _____   Date _____

Assessment Rubric: Writing Traits

Title: _____

Future Spelling Words

◎ _____

◎ _____

◎ _____

◎ _____

	Score 1	Score 2
Ideas	_____	_____
Organization	_____	_____
Word Choice	_____	_____
Conventions	_____	_____
Neatness	_____	_____
Effort	_____	_____
Total	_____	_____

4 Excellent!

3 Very nice!

2 Good job!

1 Needs improvement.

Comments: _____

_____

_____

_____

Name _____ Date _____

Assessment Rubric: Writing Traits

Title: _____

	Excellent!	Very nice!	Good job!	Needs improvement.
Ideas	4	3	2	1
Organization	4	3	2	1
Voice	4	3	2	1
Word Choice	4	3	2	1
Sentence Fluency	4	3	2	1
Conventions	4	3	2	1
Presentation	4	3	2	1

Comments: _____

_____

_____

_____

_____

_____

Trait-Based Mini-Lessons for Teaching Writing in Grades 2–4
SCHOLASTIC TEACHING RESOURCES

Assessment Rubric: Ideas, Organization, and Sentence Fluency

Title: _____

_____ Begins with a strong lead sentence.

4   3   2   1

_____ Includes details.

4   3   2   1

_____ Elaborates on ideas.

4   3   2   1

_____ Sentences flow smoothly.

4   3   2   1

_____ Ends with a closing statement.

4   3   2   1

Comments: _____

_____

_____

_____

_____

_____

4 Excellent!

3 Very nice!

2 Good job!

1 Needs improvement.

I can tell you care about your topic!

Great focus!

Grand Elaboration Award!

You included lots of details in your writing!

Effective lead!

Your conclusion left me with something to think about!

Super organization!

Incredible voice!

Trait-Based Mini-Lessons for Teaching Writing in Grades 2–4
SCHOLASTIC TEACHING RESOURCES

Awesome word choice!

I nearly believed I was there!

Super sentence fluency!

You used some interesting words!

Your sentences flow smoothly!

Your writing has spark, feeling, and commitment!

Super use of conventions!

Beautiful presentation!

Recommended Children's Books by Author

Adler, David A. *A Picture Book of Helen Keller*. New York: Holiday House, 1990.

Adoff, Arnold. *Love Letters*. New York: Blue Sky Press, 1997.

———. *Sports Pages*. New York: J. B. Lippincott, 1986.

Allard, Harry and James Marshall. *Miss Nelson Has a Field Day*. Boston: Houghton Mifflin, 1985.

———. *Miss Nelson Is Missing!* Boston: Houghton Mifflin, 1977.

Allen, Debbie. *Dancing in the Wings*. New York: Dial Books for Young Readers, 2000.

Anderson, Laurie Halse. *Thank You, Sarah! The Woman Who Saved Thanksgiving*. New York: Simon & Schuster Books for Young Readers, 2002.

Andreae, Giles. *Giraffes Can't Dance*. New York: Orchard Books, 2001.

Arnosky, Jim. *All About Turkeys*. New York: Scholastic Press, 1998.

Banyai, Istvan. *Zoom*. New York: Viking Press, 1995.

———. *Re-Zoom*. New York: Viking Press, 1995.

Baylor, Byrd. *I'm in Charge of Celebrations*. New York: Scribner's, 1986.

———. *The Table Where Rich People Sit*. New York: Scribner's, 1994.

Berger, Samantha. *Grammar Tales: When Comma Came to Town*. New York: Scholastic, 2004.

Brown, Margaret Wise. *The Important Book*. New York: Harper, 1949.

Browne, Anthony. *Willy the Wimp*. New York: Alfred A. Knopf, 1984.

Buehner, Caralyn and Mark. *The Escape of Marvin the Ape*. New York: Dial Books for Young Readers, 1992.

Bunting, Eve. *Dandelions*. San Diego: Harcourt Brace & Company, 1995.

———. *Fly Away Home*. New York: Clarion Books, 1991.

———. *Train to Somewhere*. New York: Clarion Books, 1996.

Burleigh, Robert. *Hoops*. San Diego: Silver Whistle, 1997.

Byars, Betsy. *The Summer of the Swans*. New York: Viking Press, 1970.

Byles, Monica. *Life in the Polar Lands*. New York: Franklin Watts, 1990.

Cannon, Janell. *Crickwing*. San Diego: Harcourt Brace & Company, 2000.

Charlesworth, Liza. *Grammar Tales: The No-Good, Rotten, Run-On Sentence*. New York: Scholastic, 2004.

Cherry, Lynne. *The Great Kapok Tree: A Tale of the Amazon Rain Forest*. San Diego: Harcourt Brace Jovanovich, 1990.

Cline-Ransome, Lesa. *Quilt Alphabet*. New York: Holiday House, 2001.

Coerr, Eleanor. *Sadako and the Thousand Paper Cranes*. New York: Putnam, 1977.

Coles, Robert. *The Story of Ruby Bridges*. New York: Scholastic, 1995.

Cook, Diane. *Mozart: World-Famous Composer*. Philadelphia: Mason Crest Publishers, 2003.

Cooney, Barbara. *Eleanor*. New York: Viking Press, 1996.

Cowcher, Helen. *Rain Forest*. New York: Farrar, Straus and Giroux, 1988.

Cowley, Joy. *Red-Eyed Tree Frog*. New York: Scholastic, 1999.

Cronin, Doreen. *Click, Clack, Moo: Cows That Type*. New York: Simon & Schuster Books for Young Readers, 2000.

Dahl, Roald. *James and the Giant Peach*. New York: Alfred A. Knopf, 1961.

Day, Alexandra. *Frank and Ernest*. New York: Scholastic, 1988.

DiCamillo, Kate. *Because of Winn-Dixie*. Cambridge, MA: Candlewick Press, 2000.

Dotlich, Rebecca Kai. *Lemonade Sun and Other Summer Poems*. Honesdale, PA: Wordsong/Boyds Mills Press, 1998.

Duke, Kate. *Aunt Isabel Tells a Good One*. New York: Dutton Children's Books, 1992.

Edwards, Pamela Duncan. *Barefoot: Escape on the Underground Railroad*. New York: HarperCollins, 1997.

Erdrich, Lise. *Sacagawea*. Minneapolis: Carolrhoda Books, 2003.

Fleming, Denise. *Barnyard Banter*. New York: Henry Holt & Company, 1994.

————. *In the Small, Small Pond*. New York: Henry Holt & Company, 1993.

————. *Time to Sleep*. New York: Henry Holt & Company, 1997.

————. *Where Once There Was a Wood*. New York: Henry Holt & Company, 1996.

Fleming, Maria. *Grammar Tales: The Bug Book*. New York: Scholastic, 2004.

————. *Grammar Tales: Chicken in the City*. New York: Scholastic, 2004.

————. *Grammar Tales: Tillie's Tuba*. New York: Scholastic, 2004.

————. *Grammar Tales: A Verb for Herb*. New York: Scholastic, 2004.

Florian, Douglas. *Beast Feast*. San Diego: Harcourt Brace Jovanovich, 1994.

————. *Insectlopedia: Poems and Paintings*. San Diego: Harcourt Brace & Company, 1998.

————. *Summersaults: Poems and Paintings*. New York: Greenwillow Books, 2002.

Fox, Mem. *Night Noises*. San Diego: Harcourt Brace Jovanovich, 1989.

————. *Possum Magic*. San Diego: Harcourt Brace Jovanovich, 1983.

————. *Tough Boris*. San Diego: Harcourt Brace Jovanovich, 1994.

————. *Wilfrid Gordon McDonald Partridge*. Brooklyn, NY: Kane/Miller Book Publishers, 1985.

French, Jackie. *Diary of a Wombat*. Pymble, N. S. W.: Angus & Robertson, 2002.

Freymann, Saxton and Joost Elffers. *How Are You Peeling?* New York: Scholastic, 1999.

Fritz, Jean. *Just a Few Words, Mr. Lincoln: The Story of the Gettysburg Address*. New York: Grosset & Dunlap, 1993.

George, Jean Craighead. *Look to the North: A Wolf Pup Diary*. New York: HarperCollins Publishers, 1997.

Geraghty, Paul. *Look Out, Patrick!* New York: Macmillan, 1990.

Gibbons, Gail. *Cats*. New York: Holiday House, 1996.

————. *The Moon Book*. New York: Holiday House, 1997.

————. *Penguins!* New York: Holiday House, 1998.

Giblin, James Cross. *George Washington: A Picture Book Biography*. New York: Scholastic, 1992.

Glaser, Linda. *Fabulous Frogs*. Brookfield, CT: Millbrook Press, 1999.

Gray, Libba Moore. *Little Lil and the Swing-Singing Sax*. New York: Simon & Schuster Books for Young Readers, 1996.

———. *My Mama Had a Dancing Heart*. New York: Orchard Books, 1995.

Greenfield, Eloise. *Honey, I Love and Other Love Poems*. New York: Crowell, 1978.

———. *Under the Sunday Tree*. New York: Harper & Row, 1988.

Grimes, Nikki. *Something on My Mind*. New York: Dial Press, 1978.

Guiberson, Brenda Z. *Into the Sea*. New York: Henry Holt & Company, 1996.

Hall, Donald. *I Am the Dog, I Am the Cat*. New York: Dial Books for Young Readers, 1994.

Heller, Ruth. *Behind the Mask: A Book About Prepositions*. New York: Grosset & Dunlap, 1995.

———. *A Cache of Jewels and Other Collective Nouns*. New York: Grosset & Dunlap, 1987.

———. *Chickens Aren't the Only Ones*. New York: Grosset & Dunlap, 1981.

———. *Fantastic! Wow! And Unreal! A Book About Interjections and Conjunctions*. New York: Grosset & Dunlap, 1998.

———. *Kites Sail High: A Book About Verbs*. New York: Grosset & Dunlap, 1988.

———. *Many Luscious Lollipops: A Book About Adjectives*. New York: Grosset & Dunlap, 1989.

———. *Merry-Go-Round: A Book About Nouns*. New York: Grosset & Dunlap, 1990.

———. *Mine, All Mine: A Book About Pronouns*. New York: Grosset & Dunlap, 1997.

———. *Up, Up, and Away: A Book About Adverbs*. New York: Grosset & Dunlap, 1991.

Henkes, Kevin. *Wemberly Worried*. New York: Greenwillow Books, 2000.

Hepworth, Cathi. *Antics!* New York: Putnam Publishing Group, 1992.

Hesse, Karen. *Come On, Rain*. New York: Scholastic, 1999.

Hibbert, Adam. *A Freshwater Pond*. New York: Crabtree Publishing Company, 1999.

Hoose, Philip and Hannah. *Hey, Little Ant*. Berkeley, CA: Tricycle Press, 1998.

Hopkins, Lee Bennett. *Extra Innings: Baseball Poems*. San Diego: Harcourt Brace Jovanovich, 1993.

———. *Marvelous Math: A Book of Poems*. New York: Simon & Schuster Books for Young Readers, 1997.

Hopkinson, Deborah. *Under the Quilt of Night*. New York: Atheneum Books for Young Readers, 2002.

Houston, Gloria. *My Great-Aunt Arizona*. New York: HarperCollins Publishers, 1992.

Howe, James. *It Came From Beneath the Bed! Tales From the House of Bunnicula*. New York: Atheneum Books for Young Readers, 2002.

Howker, Janni. *Walk With a Wolf*. Cambridge, MA: Candlewick Press, 1998.

James, Simon. *Dear Mr. Blueberry*. New York: Margaret K. McElderry Books, 1991.

Janeczko, Paul B. *A Poke in the I: A Collection of Concrete Poems*. Cambridge, MA: Candlewick Press, 2001.

Johnston, Tony. *Amber on the Mountain*. New York: Dial Books for Young Readers, 1994.

Jordan, Martin and Tanis. *Amazon Alphabet*. New York: Kingfisher, 1996.

Ketteman, Helen. *Armadillo Tattletale*. New York: Scholastic Press, 2000.

Khanduri, Kamini. *Polar Wildlife*. Manassas, VA: E D & C Publishing, 1993.

Kitchen, Bert. *Somewhere Today*. Cambridge, MA: Candlewick Press, 1992.

Kleven, Elisa. *The Lion and the Little Red Bird*. New York: Dutton Children's Books: 1992.

Kline, Suzy. *Horrible Harry and the Dungeon*. New York: Viking Press, 1996.

Kramer, Stephen. *Lightning*. Minneapolis: Carolrhoda Books, 1992.

Kranking, Kathleen W. *The Ocean Is . . .* New York: Henry Holt & Company, 2003.

Krensky, Stephen. *Egypt*. New York: Scholastic, 2001.

Lasky, Kathryn. *A Brilliant Streak: The Making of Mark Twain*. San Diego: Harcourt Brace & Company, 1998.

Levine, Gail Carson. *Ella Enchanted*. New York: HarperCollins Publishers, 1997.

Lewis, C. S. *The Lion, the Witch and the Wardrobe*. London: G. Bles, 1950.

L'Hommedieu, Arthur John. *Ocean Tide Pool*. New York: Children's Press, 1997.

Lobel, Arnold. *Fables*. New York: Harper & Row, 1980.

Locker, Thomas. *Cloud Dance*. San Diego: Silver Whistle, 2000.

———. *Mountain Dance*. San Diego: Silver Whistle, 2001.

———. *Water Dance*. San Diego: Harcourt Brace & Company, 1997.

London, Jonathan. *Baby Whale's Journey*. San Francisco: Chronicle Books, 1999.

———. *The Eyes of Gray Wolf*. San Francisco: Chronicle Books, 1993.

———. *Red Wolf Country*. New York: Dutton Children's Books, 1996.

Longfellow, Henry Wadsworth. "Hiawatha's Childhood" in *The Song of Hiawatha*. New York: Dandelion Press, 1979.

———. *Paul Revere's Ride*. Honesdale, PA: Boyds Mills Press, 2003.

MacLachlan, Patricia. *All the Places to Love*. New York: HarperCollins Publishers, 1994.

———. *What You Know First*. New York: HarperCollins Publishers, 1995.

Maizels, Jennie and Kate Petty. *The Amazing Pop-Up Grammar Book*. New York: Dutton Children's Books, 1996.

Mannis, Celeste Davidson. *One Leaf Rides the Wind*. New York: Viking Press, 2002.

Marshall, James. *Goldilocks and the Three Bears*. New York: Dial Books for Young Readers, 1988.

———. *Wings: A Tale of Two Chickens*. New York: Viking Kestrel, 1986.

Martin, Justin McCory. *Grammar Tales: Francine Fribble, Proofreading Policewoman*. New York: Scholastic, 2004.

———. *Grammar Tales: The Mega-Deluxe Capitalization Machine*. New York: Scholastic, 2004.

———. *Grammar Tales: The Mystery of the Missing Socks*. New York: Scholastic, 2004.

———. *Grammar Tales: The Planet Without Pronouns*. New York: Scholastic, 2004.

Mathers, Petra. *Sophie and Lou*. New York: HarperCollins Publishers, 1991.

McGovern, Ann. *If You Lived in Colonial Times*. New York: Four Winds Press, 1964.

Meddaugh, Susan. *Martha Speaks*. Boston: Houghton Mifflin, 1992.

Mochizuki, Ken. *Baseball Saved Us*. New York: Lee & Low, 1993.

Moss, Marissa. *Amelia's Notebook*. Berkeley, CA: Tricycle Press, 1995.

Munson, Derek. *Enemy Pie*. San Francisco: Chronicle Books, 2000.

Myers, Walter Dean. *Harlem: A Poem*. New York: Scholastic Press, 1997.

Naylor, Phyllis Reynolds. *Shiloh*. New York: Atheneum Books for Young Readers, 1991.

Noble, Trinka Hakes. *Meanwhile, Back at the Ranch*. New York: Dial Books for Young Readers, 1987.

Nye, Naomi Shihab. *Sitti's Secrets*. New York: Four Winds Press, 1994.

Osborne, Mary Pope. *High Tide in Hawaii: Magic Tree House #28*. New York: Random House, 2003.

Paolilli, Paul. *Silver Seeds: A Book of Nature Poems*. New York: Viking Press, 2001.

Park, Barbara. *Mick Harte Was Here*. New York: Alfred A. Knopf, 1995.

Parker, Steve. *It's an Ant's Life: My Story of Life in the Nest*. Pleasantville, NY: Reader's Digest Children's Books, 1999.

Patterson, Francine. *Koko's Kitten*. New York: Scholastic, 1985.

Paulsen, Gary. *The Tortilla Factory*. San Diego: Harcourt Brace & Company, 1995.

———. *Woodsong*. New York: Bradbury Press, 1990.

———. *Worksong*. San Diego: Harcourt Brace & Company, 1997.

Peters, Lisa Westberg. *The Sun, the Wind and the Rain*. New York: Henry Holt & Company, 1988.

Pinkney, Andrea Davis. *Duke Ellington*. New York: Hyperion Books for Children, 1998.

Polacco, Patricia. *The Bee Tree*. New York: Philomel Books, 1993.

———. *Mrs. Mack*. New York: Philomel Books, 1998.

———. *My Ol' Man*. New York: Philomel Books, 1995.

———. *Pink and Say*. New York: Philomel Books, 1994.

———. *When Lightning Comes in a Jar*. New York: Philomel Books, 2002.

Posada, Mia. *Dandelions: Stars in the Grass*. Minneapolis: Carolrhoda Books, 2000.

Prelutsky, Jack. *Tyrannosaurus Was a Beast: Dinosaur Poems*. New York: Greenwillow Books, 1988.

Pulver, Robin. *Punctuation Takes a Vacation*. New York: Holiday House, 2003.

Rappaport, Doreen. *Martin's Big Words: The Life of Dr. Martin Luther King, Jr.* New York: Hyperion Books for Children, 2001.

Raschka, Chris. *Ring! Yo?* New York: DK Ink, 2000.

———. *Yo! Yes?* New York: Orchard Books, 1993.

Resnick, Jon. *Orly the Orangutan*. Reisterstown, MD: Flying Frog Publishing, 2001.

Riddle, John. *Marco Polo*. Broomall, PA: Mason Crest Publishers, 2003.

Ringgold, Faith. *Aunt Harriet's Underground Railroad in the Sky*. New York: Crown Publishers, 1992.

———. *Tar Beach*. New York: Crown Publishers, 1991.

Rogasky, Barbara. *Winter Poems*. New York: Scholastic, 1994.

Rowling, J. K. *Harry Potter and the Sorcerer's Stone*. New York: Scholastic, 1998.

Ryan, Pam Muñoz. *When Marian Sang*. New York: Scholastic Press, 2002.

Rylant, Cynthia. *Appalachia: The Voices of Sleeping Birds*. San Diego: Harcourt Brace Jovanovich, 1991.

———. *In November*. San Diego: Harcourt Brace & Company, 2000.

———. *Missing May*. New York: Orchard Books, 1992.

———. *The Relatives Came*. New York: Bradbury Press, 1985.

———. *The Whales*. New York: Scholastic, 1996.

———. *When I Was Young in the Mountains*. New York: Dutton, 1982.

San Souci, Daniel. *North Country Night*. New York: Doubleday, 1990.

Say, Allen. *A River Dream*. Boston: Houghton Mifflin, 1988.

Scieszka, Jon and Lane Smith. *The Stinky Cheese Man and Other Fairly Stupid Tales*. New York: Viking Press, 1992.

———. *The True Story of the 3 Little Pigs*. New York: Viking Kestrel, 1989.

Shannon, David. *A Bad Case of Stripes*. New York: Blue Sky Press, 1998.

Simon, Seymour. *Sharks*. New York: HarperCollins, 1995.

———. *Stars*. New York: Morrow, 1986.

———. *Wolves*. New York: HarperCollins, 1993.

Stanley, Diane. *Raising Sweetness*. New York: Putnam's Sons, 1999.

———. *Saving Sweetness*. New York: Putnam's Sons, 1996.

Steig, William. *Amos & Boris*. New York: Farrar, Straus and Giroux, 1971.

———. *Caleb & Kate*. New York: Farrar, Straus and Giroux, 1977.

———. *Sylvester and the Magic Pebble*. New York: Windmill Books, 1969.

Stepanek, Mattie J. T. *Heartsongs*. New York: Hyperion, 2001.

Still, John. *Amazing Beetles*. New York: Alfred A. Knopf, 1991.

Stonehouse, Bernard and Esther Bertram. *The Truth About Animal Senses*. New York: Tangerine Press, 2002.

Teague, Mark. *The Secret Shortcut*. New York: Scholastic, 1996.

Thayer, Ernest Lawrence. *Casey at the Bat: A Ballad of the Republic, Sung in the Year 1888*. New York: Simon & Schuster Books for Young Readers, 2003.

Turner, Priscilla. *The War Between the Vowels and the Consonants*. New York: Farrar, Straus and Giroux, 1996.

Van Allsburg, Chris. *Jumanji*. Boston: Houghton Mifflin, 1981.

———. *The Mysteries of Harris Burdick*. Boston: Houghton Mifflin, 1984.

Venezia, Mike. *Monet*. Chicago: Children's Press, 1993.

Viorst, Judith. *Alexander and the Terrible, Horrible, No Good, Very Bad Day*. New York: Atheneum Books for Young Readers, 1972.

Waters, Kate. *Giving Thanks: The 1621 Harvest Feast*. New York: Scholastic, 2001.

———. *Sarah Morton's Day: A Day in the Life of a Pilgrim Girl*. New York: Scholastic, 1989.

White, E. B. *Charlotte's Web*. New York: Harper & Row, 1952.

———. *The Trumpet of the Swan*. New York: Harper & Row, 1970.

Wiesner, David. *Free Fall*. New York: Lothrop, Lee & Shepard Books, 1988.

———. *The Three Pigs*. New York: Clarion Books, 2001.

———. *Tuesday*. New York: Clarion Books, 1991.

Wilbur, Richard. *The Disappearing Alphabet*. San Diego: Harcourt Brace & Company, 1998.

Williams, Vera B. *A Chair for My Mother*. New York: Greenwillow Books, 1982.

Winter, Jeanette. *Follow the Drinking Gourd*. New York: Alfred A. Knopf, 1988.

Wong, Janet S. *You Have to Write*. New York: Margaret K. McElderry Books, 2002.

Wood, Audrey. *Quick as a Cricket*. New York: Child's Play-International, 1990.

Wright-Frierson, Virginia. *A Desert Scrapbook: Dawn to Dusk in the Sonoran Desert*. New York: Simon & Schuster Books for Young Readers, 1996.

Yolen, Jane. *Owl Moon*. New York: Philomel Books, 1987.

———. *Sea Watch: A Book of Poetry*. New York: Philomel Books, 1996.

Young, Ed. *Seven Blind Mice*. New York: Philomel Books, 1992.

Bibliography of Professional Resources

Culham, Ruth. *6+1 Traits of Writing: The Complete Guide, Grades 3 and Up*. New York: Scholastic, 2003.

Fletcher, Ralph. *What a Writer Needs*. Portsmouth, NH: Heinemann, 1993.

Fox, Mem. *Dear Mem Fox, I Have Read All Your Books Even the Pathetic Ones: And Other Incidents in the Life of a Children's Book Author*. San Diego: Harcourt Brace Jovanovich, 1992.

———. *Radical Reflections: Passionate Opinions on Teaching, Learning, and Living*. San Diego: Harcourt, Brace & Company, 1993.

Graves, Donald H. and Virginia Stuart. *Write From the Start: Tapping Your Child's Natural Writing Ability*. New York: Dutton, 1985.

Lane, Barry. "Quality in Writing." *Writing Teacher*, 9 (3). 3–8, 1996.